Okay, I'll get up in five seconds and go into this room. Keep an open mind, Dillon. Keep an open mind.

Dillon couldn't help but breathe hard as he sat slumped against the door.

Five.

As soon as he started the countdown, Dillon realized just how nervous he was to enter this room.

Four.

He hadn't made any movement to stand up or reach for the door handle, but he knew the countdown had to continue.

Three.

Dillon closed his eyes and felt a bead of sweat drip down his cheek.

Two.

Just as Dillon moved to slide his body up the middle of the door, someone yanked it open from the inside, and Dillon fell hard into the classroom. As he looked up into familiar eyes, he had a million more questions to ask.

WAKE UP
CALL

5 ESSENTIAL LESSONS
THEY WON'T TEACH YOU IN SCHOOL

KYLE WILLKOM

Wake Up Call

Printed in the United States of America
ISBN-13: 978-1483970738
ISBN-10: 1483970736

Learn more at:
www.KyleWillkom.com
and
www.Leadership.Focustraining.com

This book was presented to:

_____

By: _____

For: _____

Date: _____

Foreword

I first met Kyle when I was playing for the Los Angeles Clippers, and he was a manager for the Marquette Men's Basketball team. He was an energetic freshman in college who couldn't sit still for very long, his enthusiasm was contagious, and we quickly became friends. I gave him the nickname, Willy, because of his last name, and I found out in a funny conversation later that he thought I called him Willy because I didn't know his real name. Kyle and I have kept in touch long after his time as a manager came to an end, and I'm impressed to see how much he has developed over the years; not many people can call themselves published authors at his age. As a young adult I think he truly understands a student's perspective yet has the wisdom and experience needed to provide the thoughtful and important lessons shared in this book.

As a player in the NBA, I've learned about the importance of being a role model. I believe that it is important for high school students to have someone they can look up to both on and off the court. I can confidently tell you that Kyle has the personality, insight, and values needed to make a positive difference in young lives. Wake Up Call is a great book for high school students to read as Kyle's lessons are woven into an interesting and engaging story. The lessons are very clear, and the impact they can have is real. I still see ways I can apply the lessons to my life, and it's been a while since I was in high school!

I'm happy to support Kyle as he continues to be a positive influence on youth across the nation as an author and a speaker. He still has the same energy and enthusiasm that he had the first time we met.... and I still call him Willy.

Steve Novak
Shooting Guard
New York Knicks

Contents

This book is dedicated to my family:
Monte, Patti, John, Bryan, and Erin

You've been there for me from the day I was born.

Acknowledgments

To my family: Monte, Patti, John, Bryan, and Erin. Your encouragement and love has always amazed me. Thank you for everything.

To Major Washington, Lalton Bell, and Bill Zuiker. Thank you for teaching me things I could have never learned in a classroom.

To Todd, Matt, and Mel. Thank you for helping me with this project and for providing me with a second family. You've believed in me from early on, and I owe much of my success and happiness to you and the influence you've had on my life.

To the rest of the FOCUS Family. Thank you for being so extraverted. You add a spark to my life, and I'm so grateful to be a part of yours.

To Wisconsin DECA. The people I've met, lessons I've learned, and support I've received from DECA have helped me grow immensely as a writer and young professional. A special thank you to Don Patterson, Breanna Speth, Jeremy Frey, Tim Fandek, Morgan Thompson, Christine O'Neil, and the members of Wisconsin DECA Leadership Team 47, Brett, Brenna, Riley, Connor, and Gus. I've learned so much from this amazing organization, and you all have contributed a great deal to my experiences.

To those who looked over my book. Your feedback made it what it is. I owe a great deal to you all for your friendship and guidance. Thank you, specifically, to Matt, Kris, Amy, Latrell, Betsy, Tina, Valorie, Hannah, Kim, Geof, and Raquel.

To Marshfield, Wisconsin. I love you.

To Marquette University. Thank you for encouraging me to be the difference. I'm trying.

To The Brew Bayou at Marquette University. I must have gotten 30 free coffees while writing this book because of the little cutout membership cards. The atmosphere was perfect for writing, and I appreciate it.

To my friends in California who still call me Intern. You inspired me in ways you didn't realize, and I'm thankful to have met all of you.

To my headphones. I never actually had music playing, but I noticed that people wouldn't distract me when I had headphones in. I owe a great deal of focus to you.

I wish I could include names of all of my friends and coworkers from HarQen, KOHL'S, and Uline. You know who you are. Thank you for the amazing work experiences; I grew a great deal from all of them, and enjoyed my time with all of you.

To all my friends and family who have asked about the book, listened intently, encouraged my writing, and supported my progress. Thank you for helping me move forward with my dreams.

And last, but not least, thank you God, for your Son and for blessing me beyond comprehension.

Wake Up Call
Five Essential Lessons They Won't Teach You in School

Graduation

"You all have bright and beautiful futures!" The graduation speaker yelled too loudly into the microphone at the front of the old musty gym.

Dillon wondered why they held graduation in the gym every year; it was small and dimly lit, much like the high school itself, and held a very distinct odor from the countless number of sweaty basketball practices that had taken place there.

He thought back to how many times Coach Z, his basketball coach, had yelled, "Get on the line!" indicating multiple sprints were in order. Dillon was much more comfortable running sprints in basketball shorts than sitting quietly in the gym listening to Claire Adams, the valedictorian, tell his class of two hundred all about their "Bright and beautiful futures."

What a joke.

When it came to an average high school student, Dillon was it. He was good at many things, extraordinary at very few. He was good looking enough to have a couple girlfriends, but was never the guy dating the cheerleader by any means. While Dillon could name everyone in his high school, probably only half of his classmates could remember his name.

All of this was completely fine with him. He saw himself as a pretty easy-going, light-hearted guy and wasn't all too worried about what the popular girls said about him when they gathered at "the locker".

If they have ever even talked about me at the locker.

Aside from the obvious reasons to be excited about wearing a graduation cap, Dillon liked that everyone was wearing them today for two reasons; the first reason being his never-ending struggle with hair gel. He had tried everything with his hair during high school. He had shaved it off, grown it out, combed it over, spiked it up, even tried the "ski jump" where the front is spiked and the rest is matted down. He had already decided that none of these styles would be accompanying him to college. The second thing that excited Dillon about the graduation caps was seeing the clear struggle that the girls had with placing something foreign over their previously perfect hair.

Hilarious.

"We all have the potential to achieve great things!" Claire announced as she started to get emotional.

Dillon rolled his eyes and shot a sarcastic glance over to his best friend, Will, who glanced back and pretended he was falling asleep. Dillon held back a chuckle as Will pretended to struggle to keep his eyes open, then fall asleep on the shoulder of the blonde sitting next to him. She quickly jabbed him with her elbow, and he pretended to wake up like he didn't know what had happened. Dillon let out a small laugh, which drew several unhappy glances; he whispered an apology and then looked down with a smile.

"This is the first day of the rest of our lives…" Claire continued, with a tear running down her face. Dillon could not believe how stereotypical this graduation speech was. No one was crying except Claire, and her parents, but everything she said seemed like it came out of a corny romantic comedy movie.

"I believe in all of you!"

As corny as all of it was, and as much as he refused to admit it, these overused terms made Dillon a little nervous. By most people's standards, Dillon was successful in high school, both in academics and athletics, but he wasn't exactly sure how his high school successes would translate to the college scene. College would be a brand new world for him, and as eager as he was to go, there was a part of him that was uneasy about the idea.

Most of Dillon's classmates seemed excited and confident about college, and Dillon knew that to them, he seemed excited and confident about college too. He thought about how many of his classmates would drop out and be back in his small hometown before the end of their first college semester. He laughed to himself at the idea.

Most of them.

Dillon looked over at Will again.

But not Will and me.

Will had been Dillon's best friend for years. They had grown up together. Will had always been somewhat of a firework, and if half of the class remembered Dillon's name, everyone in the entire school knew Will's. The fact that he made it through high school without being expelled was amazing to Dillon.

It was not that Will did anything blatantly stupid or illegal; he was much more creative than that. Like the time Will waited for hours on the catwalk of the auditorium so that he could move the statue of the mascot into the principal's office in the middle of the night. When he got caught, there was talk of felony charges. When Dillon asked if they were going to give him *Breaking and Entering*, Will laughed and said, "First of all, I didn't *break* anything but rules...and preconceived notions that the principal is untouchable, and I don't think *entering* is a felony charge by itself. I enter this place all the time."

Dillon knew for sure that the reason Will never got in any real trouble was because of his undeniable charm. He would smile, say something witty, and the attitude in the room would change. Dillon thought about the time Will had put two hundred goldfish in the school swimming pool. Both he and Will were brought into the principal's office and questioned. When asked how his day was going, Will simply said, "Swimmingly, how is yours?" When asked if they had pulled the prank, Will said, "Look, I know the situation seems fishy, but we had no part in this…we're golden." Dillon almost laughed out loud just thinking about it, but held himself back knowing the glances he would get if he did.

"And that is why I love this school, and that is why I love all of you," Claire said, holding back her tears on the stage. Dillon looked up to his parents and smiled. He was happy that his dad had made it to his graduation. Although Dillon's dad was always traveling with work, Dillon knew he tried to be as supportive as possible when he was around.

And if Dillon's dad wasn't supportive enough, his mom made up for it in every way. She would never miss one of Dillon's home basketball games. She constantly made signs that were bright and encouraging; one time she even brought face paint to a game and convinced all the parents it was a good idea to paint their faces and look like old-school warriors in the stands; the other team's parent section didn't know what to think. Dillon's mom worked full-time, but was always home in time to make him dinner.

Sitting next to Dillon's parents were Dillon's grandma and grandpa, both of whom had retired years ago and lived for moments like this in their grandson's life. Dillon had lost his other grandparents years before. He would never forget hearing that his grandfather on his dad's side had passed away. He was in sixth grade and decided to go on a run later that day; he felt completely weightless. He ran for three miles across the town without getting tired so he decided to keep going. He ran three more miles along the city limits before deciding to turn back. He returned home after his twelve-mile run, but felt as though he had just left minutes before. Dillon always thought it was amazing how little you can pay attention to reality when something else is so heavy on your mind.

Dillon knew he should probably spend more time with his living grandparents, but he wasn't about to go out of his way to make it happen. He knew very little about them aside from the fact that they were in the military together years earlier. He sometimes wondered about how they met and what type of training they went through, but he never could remember to ask them. Even though he had always lived in the same town that they did, he found it hard to keep up with anyone who didn't have a cell phone.

How can they live without cell phones?

Scanning the old gym, Dillon's eyes fell on Mayor Davis who was sitting on the stage waiting patiently for Claire to finish. There were times when Dillon wondered how the man had become so beloved. The community would stand behind Mayor Davis through anything, and he was still a fairly young man.

I bet he becomes president someday.

Dillon looked back at the stage as Claire was finishing her speech, "Good luck to all of you; I know you're going to accomplish wonderful, amazing things."

It's about time that's over.

The principal stepped up to the stage as a woman started reading names at the podium. Mr. Rice, a guidance counselor at the high school, handed diplomas to the principal. This was the man that Dillon could always count on if he needed to have a conversation. Mr. Rice always had time to listen, and Dillon was thankful for that.

Maybe I should write him a thank you note.

One by one, students walked across the stage to shake the principal's hand and receive their diploma. When Dillon's time came to receive his diploma, he took a deep breath. This was it; this was the end of an era. He knew a million things would change in his life and receiving this diploma would be the turning point. He wasn't exactly freaking out, but he did wonder if everyone else was as uneasy about the future as he was. He strode across the stage with a smile on his face and shook the principal's hand.

"Good luck to you, son." The principal said with a smile.

Dillon heard later that the principal called every young man in the high school "son," and when Will received his diploma, he sarcastically responded, "Thanks, Dad."

When all the students got back to their seats, the principal stepped up to the microphone, and addressing everyone in the gymnasium, proclaimed, "Ladies and gentlemen, please give a round of applause for our newest graduates!" The parents erupted in applause, the band started playing the school song, and all the students threw their caps up in the air. For Dillon, the moment was surreal; he felt free from the place he had spent the last four years, and he was ecstatic.

After the ceremony, all the graduates proceeded out of the double doors of the gymnasium into the sunlight in front of the school. Dillon looked back at his high school and felt a strange sense of pride. He realized that he had never really thought about what it would feel like to graduate. He always knew it would happen, but now that it had, he couldn't decide if he was nervous for the future, proud of what he'd accomplished, or just plain excited to never have to sit through one of Mr. Harrison's boring biology lectures again. He smiled and turned to see Will coming toward him.

"Nice hair, bro!" Will yelled with a laugh.

Dillon had lost his graduation cap after throwing it up into the air, so his hair was matted down over his forehead.

"Touchy subject, Will. Watch your mouth!" Dillon shot back with a smile.

If anyone was excited to graduate, it was Will. Although Will was not a straight A student, his charisma led everyone to believe that he would be successful. No one would ever say it out loud though because Will would be the first to tell them that he's a big fish in a small pond. He was definitely ready for the next stage of his life, and high school graduation was just a small feat that he needed to get out of the way before moving on to bigger and better things.

After saying hello to several people on his way over, Will walked up and stood close to his best friend. He took the smile off his face, put his hand on Dillon's shoulder and looked down at the ground. "Hey man, I need to talk to you about something serious."

"Alright. What's going on?"

"It's just...well...wow, this is hard for me to say."

Dillon knew this had to be a joke, but he played along saying, "Come on man, you know you can tell me anything."

Will hadn't looked up from the ground and kept his hand on Dillon's shoulder, "Alright...here goes. There's a huge party tonight at Amanda's house and you're coming with." Will looked up at Dillon with his signature smile back on his face and laughed. "It's going to be off the hook!"

Dillon laughed and shook his head, "You know I'm not going to that."

Will acted surprised. "What?! Why? If there is ever a time to attend an event, the time is now. Plus," Will lied, "I heard Amanda is feelin' you!"

"Now we both know you're lying."

"Alright, you got me on that one, but give me one reason that you don't want to come."

Dillon looked at Will as if the answer was obvious. "How about getting busted? You know that cops are going to be looking for underage drinkers after graduation."

"Yea...but we're faster than the cops and you know it."

Dillon laughed and said, "I'm going to have to pass; I'll give you a ride home though, just call me when you're ready to leave."

Will sarcastically pretended to be overly enthusiastic about the offer. "Wow, you would do that? Gee Dillon, you're so thoughtful!"

"Shut up," Dillon laughed.

"You sure, bro?" Will asked as a last attempt to change Dillon's mind. "Life as we know it is coming to an end. I think that's a reason to celebrate."

"I'll celebrate with you some other time." Dillon had never been a big partier; he had been to a couple parties in high school but knew that if he were ever caught he'd be suspended from sports.

If a student gets suspended from athletics for drinking, everyone in the entire city will talk about it.

Dillon didn't want to risk getting caught or subjecting himself to the town gossip.

Will shrugged. "Suit yourself."

"Besides," Dillon continued, "This party life is going to catch up to you at some point." Dillon smirked and jiggled his stomach indicating that Will would get a beer belly.

"Ha! Not anytime soon! I have a solid reason to think everything will be just fine."

Dillon gave Will an incredulous look. "Oh yea? What's that?"

Will smiled and took his lucky coin out of his pocket. Dillon couldn't remember a time when he saw Will without it. Dillon rolled his eyes. "You know that thing doesn't have any special powers or anything, right?"

Will pretended to be surprised and disappointed. "Really? Oh man, what am I going to do now?"

"You know what I mean. You act like it's magic. You'd be better off going to the gas station around the corner and spending that coin on some gum in case things go well for *you* with Amanda!"

Will laughed, "So Dillon does have a sense of humor after all!"

Dillon saw his parents and grandparents walking toward them. "Look, call me tonight when you need a ride, alright? I'll keep my phone on."

Will smiled and nodded as Dillon's parents made it to them. Dillon's mom pulled him in for a long hug as his dad shook Will's hand.

"We're so proud of you," Dillon's mother whispered into his ear as she ended the embrace.

Dillon didn't really know what to say. He knew that although his parents were proud of him now, they were more proud that he was headed to Marquette University in Milwaukee, Wisconsin in three months. For Dillon, the proud of you statement by his mom was more of a, "We're so proud of what you're going to do." It had always seemed a given that Dillon would attend college; he was smart enough, and always had an ambition to be successful. He just wondered how the time had already come for him to go.

I don't know if I'm ready.

He definitely knew that going to college would lead to him achieving a higher level of success; he just wished there wasn't so much pressure on it. He smiled and said thank you to his mom.

While the pressure of choosing a college added stress to Dillon's life, the fact that he and Will had decided to be roommates at Marquette eased his mind. While location, size, and academic reputation played a role in his college decision, a big part of his choice was about Will. It was comforting to know he would have his best friend with him through all of the changes that were coming.

After what seemed like a lifetime of conversations and hugs with classmates and parents, Dillon finally made it to the parking lot to head home. He looked back one last time at his high school.

Thanks for the memories.

He wondered for a second what it would look like in ten, or fifteen, or twenty years. He thought about the teachers who had an impact on his education and wondered if he had made any sort of impact on them. He thought about all his classmates; some he would miss, some he most definitely would not. He thought about Will's pranks and wondered how much more creative they would be in college. He took a moment to reminisce, then got into his car and drove home.

Dillon got home exhausted from all the excitement of graduation day. He walked up the stairs to his room and launched himself onto his bed. He pulled his phone out of his pocket and made sure the ringer was on loud so he was ready for Will's call, and placing the phone next to his face, he fell asleep.

Wake Up Call

The phone rang louder than Dillon thought it would. He buried his head deeper into his pillow to avoid the annoying ringtone he had been too lazy to change. He let it ring a few times before grabbing it, and answered with his eyes still closed.

"Will, what's up?" He said in a haze.

Dillon was surprised when the voice on the other end was not Will's. "Dillon, it's your mother…" It wasn't unusual for her to call him from work.

"Oh," Dillon said, still with his eyes closed.

Dillon's mom paused a second. "Were you still asleep?"

Dillon was confused by the comment.

What time is it?

He opened his eyes to see the sun shining through his window. He wondered if he had somehow missed Will's call from the night before, but remembering how loud his ringtone was that morning, he quickly erased the thought from his mind.

Will must have gotten a ride home from somebody else.

Dillon's mom started to talk again, slowly and seriously. "Dillon, I have to tell you something."

Now Dillon was awake. Still incredibly confused, but awake. His mom never talked like this unless there was something wrong. He had only heard that tone of voice from her once before when his grandfather had passed away. A million thoughts of what could be wrong crossed Dillon's mind.

"What's going on?"

"Last night…Will was hit by a drunk driver…and passed away." Dillon's mom said the words slowly and gently. She was trying to be sensitive, but she knew there was no good way to relay the information.

The words hit Dillon hard. He didn't know how to respond. He was in a state of shock and couldn't bring himself to react at all.

"…What?" Was all that Dillon could say, hoping his mom was joking or he had somehow misunderstood; he knew that it was neither.

His mom waited for a moment. "…I'm so sorry. I didn't want to tell you over the phone, but I didn't want you hearing from anyone else."

His first thought was one of disbelief.

What? He was supposed to call me. Why didn't he call me? I would have picked him up!

There was silence on the other end of the phone as the news started to sink in. As the reality of Will's death became clearer in Dillon's mind, he started to move from shock and disbelief to an emotional hysteria. Although the confusion was still there, he knew that none of the questions he could ask would be able to bring his best friend back. Tears welled up in Dillon's eyes as he started to think about never seeing Will again or joking around with him about pranks, and girls, and his lucky coin.

Dillon started to breathe hard as he tried to keep the tears from falling. He sat up on the edge of his bed and held the phone closely to his ear waiting for his mom to say something, anything. She didn't. When the first tear fell, he watched it as if it were happening in slow motion. He felt like a piece of his life was falling with the tear. Everything he knew and was used to was coming to an end as the tear was dropping. High school was over; Will was gone.

I can't handle this.

Dillon lifted his hand to catch the tear as it continued to fall. A part of him was hoping that it would never really reach his hand; he imagined time moving in reverse, the tear moving back to his eye, falling back to sleep, rewinding all the way back to Will's hand on his shoulder after the graduation ceremony. But as much as he wished for time to reverse, nothing he could think of could stop the tear from crashing downward. He caught it in his hand and looked at it for a second. He felt as though a million memories had built up in that tear, and when it burst onto his palm, the full gravity of the situation finally hit him, and he completely broke down. Tears streamed down his face as the vision of Will laughing next to him in his graduation gown the day before replayed in his mind. Everything had happened so fast. Dillon suddenly felt a strong sense of guilt.

What if I would have gone to the party? Everything would be different. Will would be fine. He'd be here. He'd be alive. This is my fault!

Dillon couldn't remember the last time he had cried, but he could not stop these tears, and he didn't care. His mom broke the silence on the phone as Dillon openly wept.

"I'm so sorry, Dillon." It was clear she was searching for words. "There's nothing I can say that will make this situation better; I know how close you two were. But I'm here for you...I'll always be here for you. You know that, right?"

Dillon couldn't even think about responding through his sobs. There was another short silence, before his mom spoke again.

"I'm going to come home from work. I shouldn't have told you this on the phone. I'm so sorry. I'll be there soon. I love you. Hang in there, okay?"

All of Dillon's classmates went to the wake and funeral; Dillon hadn't thought he'd be seeing them all again so soon, especially in these circumstances. Claire offered her condolences, and Dillon was a little surprised at how sincere she seemed, though it still didn't comfort him.

It seemed as though everyone in the entire town had come to say their farewells. Mr. Rice, the guidance counselor, made sure Dillon knew he would be there for him anytime. Coach Z didn't say much, but gave Dillon a hug that was probably the most meaningful moment of the day. Even Mayor Davis showed up briefly.

The days following the tragic news were the longest days of Dillon's life. Every aspect of his life had changed in dramatic ways and the gravity of the situation was overwhelming. The safety and comfort of high school was gone and his best friend had passed away. The way Dillon viewed the world was slowly changing too. The jokes that once made him fall on the ground in laughter weren't funny anymore. Whenever he would think about doing something fun or creative in town, he would always end up reminiscing about the same activities he had done in the past with Will.

It wouldn't be the same.

Dillon remembered the time he and Will wanted to set up a scavenger hunt. In realizing that they couldn't participate if they made the clues, they decided to make it a competition. They invited friends, organized two teams, and had each team make clues and tasks for the other. After one night of this competitive scavenger hunt, it was the talk of the school. Dillon and Will started to hold these competitive scavenger hunts nearly every weekend. On Easter weekend, they had each team hide Easter eggs around the town for the other team to find. Some weekends, they decided not to have clues at all, only funny tasks that the other team would have to complete at different places in the town.

Take a picture with a goose.
Take a picture imitating a statue.

14

Dance like a ballerina for 5 minutes in the McDonald's parking lot.

It was easy for Dillon to smile when remembering times like these, but the memories always ended with the realization that Will was gone and things would never be the same. Some of Dillon's friends would call and invite him to go on a scavenger hunt like the old days, but he would decline because he couldn't see it being any fun without Will.

There wasn't much that Dillon got excited about anymore. He didn't want to admit to anyone that he was somewhat depressed, but it started to get to the point where everyday tasks like getting out of bed in the morning felt like chores. The positive, easy-going attitude that he had embodied throughout high school had left him along with Will.

The next two months passed extremely slowly. Each day felt like a week, and each week felt like a year.

The changes in Dillon's life had given him a lot of time to think, and when he wasn't reminiscing about times when life was good, he was thinking about his future. His stomach would get queasy when thinking about college. He had been second-guessing his ability to excel in college even before Will had passed away; now, his failure seemed imminent.

We were supposed to be there for each other every step of the way.

The thought of moving away from home made him uneasy, and thinking about meeting new friends was unfathomable. He thought more and more about not attending college; he wasn't sure what he would do otherwise, but handling the changes college would throw at him wasn't high on his priority list.

My life has changed enough in the last two months, hasn't it?

Dillon tried not to talk about it, but he knew that a piece of himself had died with Will. His confidence was gone, his sense of humor had faded, and his positive disposition had turned to a depression that he couldn't shake.

I can't go to college.

Negotiation

Dillon sat with his parents at the dinner table three weeks before college was scheduled to start. It was quiet and everyone focused more on their food than each other.

"The potatoes are delicious." His dad tried to make small talk. No one responded.

Dillon's parents, his mom especially, did everything they could to cheer him up, but there was only so much they could do. His mom would try to spark conversations, but Dillon didn't feel like opening up. To him, every question she asked sounded like she was being nosey. Normal questions like, "How was your day?" sounded more like, "We're worried about you. Say something, anything." He felt like dinnertime had turned into a daily intervention, and he felt more comfortable keeping to himself.

However, that day was different. He needed to talk to them, but he didn't know how to break the silence that had become so typical after losing Will. In one way, he knew that what he needed to tell them was important and couldn't be avoided, but in another way, he felt that maybe he could avoid the conversation forever and everything would work itself out. Dillon built up his confidence in his head.

If I'm going to tell them, it has to be now.

"I'm not going to college." The statement cut through the silence, and he was relieved to have finally gotten it off his chest.

There was another long silence as he stared down at his food. He hadn't touched his potatoes, but started to play with them awkwardly with his fork as he waited for his parents to respond. Although he felt like his mind was made up, he was anxious to hear what his parents had to say.

Will they be upset? Will they make me go?

His mom looked up at her husband. Dillon sheepishly glanced up at his father too. It felt like minutes had passed when Dillon's father finally swallowed the food that he had been chewing. He slowly pulled the napkin off of his lap and wiped his mouth.

His father started to speak, but instead of the angry, upset tone that Dillon was ready for, his words were soft and understanding.

"Dillon, I know things have been difficult for you. Trust me, I do, and I know I haven't been around much to talk about things with you. It's not an easy thing to bring up…well, you know that already."

There was a pause before he continued. "I never told you this, but I lost a good friend of mine when I was in seventh grade. His name was John O'Reilly. He had lived across the street from me growing up, and we always played football in his backyard." He paused again, remembering his old friend. "His parents had taken him on a camping trip to Michigan, and their car slipped on some ice on the way home and rolled into a ditch. Even though his parents had reminded him, John wasn't wearing his seatbelt and died at the hospital a few hours later."

Dillon's father looked directly at Dillon. "I still think about John. I wonder if we would still call each other and ask 'how are things?' But at some point, I had to move on from thinking that my life would stay the same after he died. I had to accept that he was gone, and that all I could do was move forward, and make the best decisions that I could."

Dillon waited a moment to make sure his father had finished. "What if the best decision for me is to not go to college?"

"Well," his father hadn't broken eye contact, "That is a decision that you need to think long and hard about, but as your parents, we'll support you either way."

Dillon felt a huge sense of relief. His father had always been the strict one. Whenever Dillon would get caught for the mischief he and Will would get into, his father would always be the one telling him how irresponsible the decisions he was making were. His father was always the one to punish him, which is why Dillon had a small sense of fear when it came to communicating with him.

If I can convince him I'm not ready for college, I can convince anyone.

Dillon looked back down at his food and stabbed a small piece of chicken with his fork. He pulled it up and took his first bite of the meal. As he chewed, he looked over at his mom.

Dillon's mom had always been the one to comfort him after Dillon's father would ground him or get a little physical with his punishment. She was much more gentle than his father, and Dillon couldn't remember a single time that she had raised her voice at him.

This is going to be a breeze.

To Dillon's surprise, she started to talk the way Dillon thought his father would! She was not gentle or soft, she was strong and decided, "No, you're not making this decision yet."

Dillon stopped chewing, "What?"

"You can't make this decision yet. You haven't talked to us about this once. Yes, you're going through a tough time, and we realize that, but you can't make a rash decision about not attending college just because Will is gone."

Dillon had no idea how to respond. He waited for a moment, and found himself looking back down at his food.

He managed to murmur, "Well, what do you want me to do?"

"Think about it." She started to sound a little more understanding, "But don't just come to us tomorrow and tell us that you thought about it; I mean really think about it. Is this a decision that you actually want to make for *your* future, or are you just trying to avoid moving on?"

Dillon's father stood up. "I hate to run out on this conversation, but I have to get some work done tonight." He walked to the other side of the table and kissed Dillon's mom on the top of her head. He put one hand on Dillon's shoulder and patted Dillon on the chest with the other. "We're here for you, buddy. Keep your head up. I'm sure you'll make a good decision."

As he left the room, Dillon stood up.

"Where are you going?" His mom interjected.

"I'm finished. I'm going to my room."

"This conversation is not over." She looked at him as if it was a question, and in a way, Dillon knew it was. He knew that he could make the decision to not attend college at anytime. He knew that despite the stern voice and solid eye contact, his mom could not keep him from making the decision if it was truly what he wanted to do, but at this point, he wasn't in the mood to argue. When he sat down to dinner, he was certain that he wasn't meant for college, but something in his father's story and his mom's harsh words had convinced him that he had a lot more thinking to do.

"Alright," Dillon conceded, "I won't make the decision yet, but I don't know what's going to change in the next couple days." He walked away from the table, still pretty certain that college was not his next step. He wondered how long he would have to wait before telling his parents that he had thought about it, and that it wasn't going to happen.

That night, he didn't think about college or the dinner conversation at all. In fact, he went to his friend Amy's house for a movie with a group of friends. Although it would have bothered him in high school, he didn't mind that everyone was drinking beers as they hung out. There was no athletic code to follow anymore, and there was really no chance that cops would bust into a party where eight young people were watching a movie.

Even if they do, I'm not drinking anything.

Dillon was surprised that through the course of the night, no one brought up Will. No one asked if he was doing okay or if he was getting over it. No one looked concerned when they talked to him. No one even mentioned college. It was the first night in months that Dillon could live in the moment and get his mind off of everything.

He said goodbye to his friends as the night drew to a close. They were moderately drunk at this point and begged him to stay a little longer. He laughed and politely declined.

Amy pointed at him and yelled across the room, "We're hanging out again soon!"

Dillon smiled and said, "Count on it."

He drove home, and as he got back to his bedroom, he realized that he hadn't done any thinking about the decision that he needed to make.

I'll sleep on it.

He was still in jeans and a t-shirt, but he didn't care as he jumped into his bed and buried his face in the pillow. He struggled to pull his phone out of his pocket and place it on his pillow, and then he fell asleep.

Dillon's ringtone blasted next to his nose, and he almost jumped out of his bed. It was like one of those dreams when you're falling, and you wake up before you hit the ground. Dillon wondered if anyone ever actually hit the ground during falling dreams.

It's impossible. You always wake up!

He looked down at his phone to see his mom calling. She somehow was always able to wake him up with a phone call.

This woman has the worst timing in the world.

"Hey mom." Dillon tried hard to sound like he'd been awake for a while.

"Oh, I'm sorry, did I wake you?" She joked, knowing that her son was not awake this early on a Saturday morning.

"No, I'm good. What's up?"

"After we talked last night, I felt like I needed to help you think about your decision a little bit, but I didn't really know how…"

Dillon wasn't sure where she was going with this.

"So I called the university and told them a little about the situation."

Dillon was not happy to hear this at all. He didn't want Marquette to know that he was second-guessing his decision to attend school there. He wanted his decision to stay within his family, and let Marquette know when the time was right. His mom was going to continue talking, but he interrupted her.

"Why?"

His mom could tell that he was upset. Her tone softened, but she continued as if he had never interrupted.

"They told me that one of the best things we could do was set up a meeting with someone in the Admissions office-"

"I can't believe you would do this."

She continued again as if he didn't say anything. "And just have a conversation about what you're thinking. They won't try to persuade you of anything; they'll just help you find some direction."

Whenever someone says they won't try to persuade me, it means they're going to try to persuade me.

Dillon didn't say anything, but his mom could tell he was upset. Even knowing this, she didn't alter her train of thought.

"I set up a time for you to meet with an Admissions officer on Monday."

Dillon was not convinced by any means.

"I set it up because I think they can give you more insight than I can."

Dillon started to calm down but remained silent.

There is no way I'm going to this meeting.

Just as Dillon was deciding which excuse to give his mom as to why he wasn't interested in attending the meeting, she said maybe the only words that could change his mind.

"Just go to this meeting on Monday, and if you still think that you're not meant for college afterward, I won't say anything more about it."

Dillon thought about the proposition. He could go to the meeting with his mind made up, come back home, and not have to continue convincing his mom that college wasn't right for him. It sounded like a fair deal; one that would save him a lot of hassle if everything went as planned.

"Alright, deal. But you really can't try to talk me into anything after the meeting. Once I make up my mind, that's the final decision."

"Deal." She went back into the details of the meeting and made sure Dillon wrote everything down so he wouldn't forget. When she was sure that he had all the information he needed, she said, "Hey, I have to get back to work, but I'll be home to make you dinner."

"Alright, see you tonight."

Dillon laid back down on his bed, thinking about the meeting that his mom had set up. He started to dread the thought of it, and planned the ways that he could convince whoever it was that he was meeting with that he wasn't right for college. He had run through the obvious reasons many times before, so he started making up ridiculous reasons in his head.

I have bad breath; no one will want to hang out with me. I'm allergic to cafeteria food. I heard everyone at Marquette plays weird farm animal games online.

He laughed to himself before taking a deep breath and shook his head. The meeting was two days away, and Dillon had no idea what to expect.

The Meeting

Dillon was actually a little nervous. He was slightly more confident than he had been at the dinner conversation three days prior, but the butterflies in his stomach were still noticeable. It didn't help his nerves at all that he had a three-hour drive to Milwaukee to have this meeting at Marquette.

It will be fine...then all of these conversations can be over.

Dillon cranked up the radio when Kanye West's new song came on, and started to calm down a little bit as he tried to rap along. He would never try to sing or rap anything in front of anyone else, but alone in his car he may as well *have been* Kanye West. He remembered a TV show where cameras were hidden in cars, and people were caught belting out songs. Just at the thought, he scanned his dashboard for any hidden cameras, then smiled and continued to rap.

The Marquette University exit came faster than he had expected. As he drove past some of the buildings on the campus, he thought about the time he and Will took a tour. The tour guide was a sophomore named Jim who was incredibly outgoing. Dillon could have seen himself and Will becoming good friends with Jim. Getting a tour from someone outgoing and fun definitely played a role in Dillon and Will's college decision.

People were throwing Frisbees and socializing outside as his car moved through campus. It was a beautiful summer day, and a part of Dillon wanted to skip his meeting and go throw a Frisbee with these people.

I need to get this meeting over with.

He drove past the building where his meeting would be twice just to make sure he had the right place, and then found a parking spot.

Walking into the Marquette Admissions building, Dillon's nervousness started to come back. The fact that he was early didn't help because the woman at the counter had him take a seat in the empty office.

I should have walked around for a while...then I wouldn't have to just sit here for twenty minutes.

Dillon grabbed a magazine from the table to the side of his chair as people walked in and out of the office; some were clearly student tour guides. It was easy to tell because they all had similar charisma to Jim's. There were other students walking in and out as well, but Dillon didn't know who they were. He made it a point not to make eye contact with anyone as he waited for his meeting.

"Dillon, my boy!" The cheerful voice came from the hallway behind where Dillon was sitting. He turned around to an unexpected sight. The man standing before him was dressed in a purple suit jacket and a green bow tie. He had lighter beige dress pants on, and brown shoes that looked brand new.

Is this a joke?

The man was probably around forty-years-old, but he had a smile that made him look much younger. He had curly blonde hair that was pulled back behind his ears. His hair wasn't long; it seemed the perfect length to be youthful but still hold a professional job.

Would that be considered a mullet?

Dillon's nerves had gone away. There was no way a man in a purple jacket and green bow tie was going to convince him that college was the right path. Dillon started to wonder whether the man in front of him had attended college.

If that is where college is going to get me, I'm definitely not interested.

The man clapped his hands once and said with a smile, "Let's get this meeting started, huh?"

Dillon smiled both at the man's appearance and his mannerisms. It was clear that he was excited to be there. Dillon stood up and started to walk toward the man.

Before seeing him, Dillon had thought this meeting would consist of a long, serious conversation, but now he wasn't so sure. He had pictured a man in a suit leading him back to an office, sitting down in uncomfortable seats, and giving him a spiel.

"Martin Martins, call me either one, they're the same anyway. Pleasure to meet you." The man reached out his hand enthusiastically and shook Dillon's.

You have two first names?

As if reading Dillon's mind, Martin said, "Yes, it's true, I have two first names. My parents thought they were pretty funny. Looking back," there was a strange reminiscent look on his face for a split second. "They were pretty funny." The smile returned to his face. "Where would you like to have the meeting?"

Dillon wasn't sure what he meant, "What?"

"You know, the meeting? The one you're here for? Oh no..." Martin's face looked cleverly concerned. "Did no one tell you that you had a meeting today? You must be so confused!" He looked at the receptionist. "Someone get this boy a glass of water before he goes into shock!"

Dillon laughed out loud at how ridiculous this man was.

"Wait a second," Martin spoke very fast, "If you didn't know about this meeting, there would be no reason for you to be here so your confusion toward my question must have stemmed from the concept that we can have this meeting anywhere you'd like." Although the words flew out of his mouth quickly, Dillon was surprised at how charming and intelligent they seemed. "You're in charge, boss, we can have this meeting in my office, on the grass, on the sidewalk, in a class."

Dillon smiled at the rhyme. It reminded him of when his parents read him *Green Eggs and Ham* when he was little.

We could have this meeting here or there, we could have it anywhere.

Dillon finally responded, "Well, I guess I hadn't really thought about it."

Martin interjected quickly, "Most people rarely do, and to be honest, that's probably a good thing. The setting of the meeting should be secondary to the content for which the meeting was originally organized to discuss." It was hard for Dillon to take Martin very seriously; his mind seemed to work three times faster than a normal human being, but it also seemed impossible to dislike the man. "Let's take a walk around campus."

Martin led the way out of the Admissions Office into the warm sunlight outside. Dillon felt surprisingly comfortable. This was by no means what he had envisioned taking place at the meeting he had been dreading for the last three days.

"So, Dillon," Martin was looking upward as if he was soaking up the sunshine. His words came out slower and more naturally, but still cheerful. "I hear you're having some second thoughts about college."

Dillon responded defensively. "I just don't think I'm right for it. It's nothing against Marquette or anything; I just don't think I am meant for the whole college student thing."

"Hey there, slow down," Martin said with a smile still on his face. "I'm not here to persuade you of anything." His tone was still extremely light-hearted. "I know I look really mean, but I left my boxing gloves in my office." Dillon smiled, and Martin continued. "I just want you to be honest with me, and I'll be honest with you, and at the end of the day you can make any decision that you would like. That's the beauty of growing up. People stop telling you what to do and start responding to the choices that you make on your own."

Dillon wasn't extremely surprised to hear him say this. He knew that the college decision was his alone. As they stopped walking and waited for traffic to pass, Dillon looked up at the church that was towering over them across the street, and Martin noticed him looking.

"That's Gesu." Martin looked up at the church as if it was one of the Seven Wonders of the World, but didn't say anything more about it. Dillon found it funny that Martin hadn't been telling him anything about Marquette's campus.

The worst tour guide I've ever seen.

In a way, Dillon realized that it was nice that Martin wasn't giving historical facts about all of the old buildings. He had already heard them on his first tour of campus.

Martin and Dillon started to cross the street and Martin casually continued with his original line of questions. "So where do your hesitations lie?"

Dillon was feeling much more comfortable with Martin, but not comfortable enough to mention anything about Will. "I just don't think I'm ready." He paused for a second, "I'm not outgoing enough to make new friends. I'm not smart enough to handle college courses."

"Hmm…Okay." Martin responded, still looking up at Gesu as if these were completely valid reasons. Dillon had responded very seriously, and he was used to his parents telling him that he would make new friends easily and he wouldn't have any problems excelling academically. Hearing Martin respond nonchalantly was strange for him.

Martin stopped walking for a moment, still looking up, "There are fire alarms on the outside of the church. I never noticed that before. Wouldn't you think the people inside would need to be the first to know about a fire?"

Dillon laughed at the complete change of subject. He couldn't believe how carefree Martin seemed to be. He decided to bring the conversation back to the question that was asked of him. "College just doesn't seem like a good fit for me."

Martin started walking again. "What would you do if you didn't go to college?"

Dillon thought for a second; he knew the question was unavoidable but he hadn't really prepared for it like he should have. He could have made something up, but he decided to tell Martin the truth. "Honestly, I don't know. I think I would have some time at home to figure it out, but I don't have any real ideas right now."

Martin pointed up to a gray structure. "That's the business building. You're interested in business, right?"

"Yea, I think so." Dillon was starting to get used to the light-hearted nature of the conversation. It was clear that Martin realized the importance of asking serious questions, but didn't want to spend too much time having a downer of a conversation.

Martin sat down on a bench in front of the building and Dillon followed his lead. "You know, Dillon, you're not the only person who has doubts before college. I remember when I was your age, and I had a similar conversation with my parents that you had with yours. I sat there in my purple jacket," Martin looked at Dillon to make sure he caught the sarcasm. Dillon rolled his eyes at the thought of Martin wearing a purple suit jacket and green bow tie in high school. "And I didn't think that I was ready."

There was a long silence as Martin held eye contact with Dillon. The story did interest Dillon. "So what did you do?"

"Someone set up something really special for me; it was something that revolutionized my thought processes and overpowered any sense of doubt that had been dwelling in my mind. It was an experience that changed my life."

Dillon waited for Martin to continue, but Martin sat for a moment looking off into the distance as if he were remembering the experience that he had. Dillon couldn't take the silence. "What was the experience?"

29

"Well," Martin re-established eye contact and raised his eyebrows, "It was an experience that I was hoping to set up for you."

The words sank in for a moment, and Dillon waited for Martin to continue.

"There is one thing that you would have to agree to if I'm to do this for you." Martin made sure he had Dillon's complete attention before continuing, "You have to attend all of your courses on the first day of college."

Dillon was confused. "What? I just told you that I don't think I'm ready." He shook his head and looked at the ground.

Martin responded slowly but sped up with a smirk on his face as he continued. "I know you did, and as I mentioned before, it is completely your choice. I can't promise you that you will want to attend college after the first day, and if you don't, then you can make the decision to never attend another college course again. All I can promise you is that it will be a special experience that you will remember for the rest of your life."

"All I have to do is show up for one day?"

"That is all!" Martin was enthusiastic about his proposal, but Dillon still had questions running through his mind.

"What is going to be so special about it?"

"If I told you, it would be far less special, don't you think?" Martin's words hung in the air as Dillon took a moment before asking another question.

"And I just have to go to class on the first day?"

"You're really catching on now!" Martin said with a wink. "You'll have one day to make your decision, and I can promise you that your direction will become clear."

Dillon started to seriously think about the proposition.

It's not like I have to commit to going to college the entire year, just one day.

More than anything, Dillon's curiosity was peaked.

What could he possibly set up that I will remember for the rest of my life?

Dillon spent a minute mulling it over, and after deliberating, he could hardly believe the words that came out of his mouth. "Okay, I'll do it. I'll go to the first day."

Martin smiled. "Splendid."

"But I don't want you thinking that I'm committing to attending school here for the whole year. I'm giving it one day, just because I'm curious. I will most likely go back home after the first day."

Martin's kind expression didn't change. "Deal."

There was a short silence before Martin stood up. "Well, I'm going to head into the business building and say hi to a few people. Do you have any other questions or need anything else?"

Dillon shook his head. "I think I'm good."

"More important question, do you remember where you parked?"

Dillon laughed and nodded.

Martin reached out and shook Dillon's hand. "Feel free to walk around the campus more if you'd like. I'm no good at being a tour guide, but it would be a shame to get back in your car right away on this gorgeous day."

Dillon smiled. "Sounds good."

As Martin walked into the business building, Dillon continued to sit on the bench outside. He thought about what he had just agreed to; it was definitely going to make it more difficult to convince his parents that he wasn't ready for college after attending the first day of classes.

I wonder what the experience will be like.

Dillon started to reminisce about Will again. He didn't know why his thoughts always had to end up back at these memories. The thought of Will's funeral made him uncomfortable, and he tried to shake the image from his head. He knew that the hurt he still felt about Will's death was affecting him in a very real way, but he didn't know how to overcome it.

He couldn't sit on the bench anymore. He felt sick to his stomach like he had so many times before when thinking about the loss of Will. He got up and walked back to his car, trying hard to concentrate on what lies in front of him.

So I have to attend one day of college. I can handle that.

He got back into his car and drove home.

Decision Day

The first day of college approached faster than Dillon had anticipated. He thought that he would be counting the days, and not in a good way, until he had to pack up and leave, but the first day of classes came before any time seemed to pass at all.

After explaining what happened in the meeting with Martin, Dillon convinced his parents to drop him off at college the morning that his classes were to begin, even though most of the freshman had moved into their dorm rooms over a week earlier. He had told Martin that he would attend the first day of classes, and that was all he intended to do. He wasn't thinking about meeting people or making friends; he was interested in keeping his end of the deal. Since he was moving his things into the dorm the morning that classes began, Dillon had missed all of freshman orientation.

What does it matter? I'll only be here one day.

Dillon definitely did not pack for an entire semester of college. He had wanted to pack for one day, but his mom made him bring clothes for at least two weeks. He had brought his computer, bed sheets, a pillow, and some toiletry items, but that was about it.

Dillon's mom had also tried to talk him into moving in the day before classes began so they wouldn't have such an early morning of driving in the car, but Dillon was adamant about his decision. He'd do what he had agreed to and no more, which in Dillon's mind, made perfect sense.

People don't lose a five-dollar bet and pay someone ten. Why would I do more than I agreed to?

As his mother drove, Dillon started to think about what the first day might hold for him. Martin said it would be a special experience, but he wondered how special it could actually be considering he would only be attending one day of classes.

How life-changing can five classes be?

Dillon's mom made casual conversation as they drove. "What are you most excited about for the first day?"

"For it to be over," Dillon responded sarcastically.

"You're such a downer!" His mom gave him a quick smile as she drove. "Seriously, though, there has to be something you're looking forward to."

Dillon gave up his sarcastic front. "I guess I'm just curious to see what Martin has set up for me. I mean, I don't think it's going to change my mind about anything, but he said I'll remember it forever."

His mom nodded. "I'm excited to hear what he's set up for you too." She paused for a moment, then smiled. "Is it just me, or is there something different about Martin? The conversation we had on the phone while I was setting up your meeting was pretty interesting."

Dillon let out a little chuckle. "Yea, I don't know. I like him though."

There was a short pause before Dillon's mom said, "Me too."

The Marquette University exit made Dillon's stomach turn a little. He was definitely nervous, but he made sure his mom only saw a confident young man firm in the decision that he had already made. He acted like attending the first day of college was no big deal because he would be back home later that day.

His mom, on the other hand, started tearing up before they even saw Dillon's dorm.

Dillon looked at her like she was crazy. "Hey, I'll be home tonight. Don't worry about it."

Together, they moved a few things into Dillon's single dorm room. The thought of moving anything into a dorm room without Will made Dillon feel queasy. He *was* happy that the university didn't put him with a random roommate after Will passed away. He wanted to talk to as few people as possible before turning around and going home.

As he was moving his things into his room, Dillon noticed that he hadn't seen one person on the Marquette campus.

People must sleep in around here.

Dillon walked his mom back to the car. It was clear to him that she was trying hard to hold back tears. He understood why she would get emotional if he was leaving for good, but he wasn't planning on being gone more than a day!

"Mom, it's going to be okay."

A couple tears slowly rolled down his mom's cheeks. "Dillon, there's a million things that I feel like I never said to you, or maybe said to you but not enough, like how much I love you. I realize how many things I would do and say differently if I had the chance. I just want you to know that, no matter what you decide, you're an amazing young man, and I'm so proud of who you've become."

Dillon was still pretty calm. "Thanks, mom."

Dillon's mom wiped her tears away with her hand and smiled at her son through reddened eyes. "I need to go before I completely lose it."

They both laughed, and Dillon comforted her. "It's going to be alright."

Dillon realized this had been the first time he comforted someone after Will passed away. Before today, everyone had been worried about him, and made sure they were there for him if he needed help or comfort. It felt a little strange to be telling his mom that things would be okay after hearing it so many times in the past few months, and not believing it himself.

He gave his mom a long hug, and she made sure to say, "I love you," one last time before getting back in the car.

Dillon walked back into his dorm room and sat on his bed. It was not comfortable at all.

So this is college, huh?

He spent several minutes daydreaming about the experience ahead of him. He had already reviewed all kinds of scenarios in his mind, and he knew most of them were not possible, but at this point, it was hard for him to rule anything out.

What if Martin sets up a laser tag competition or a basketball tournament?

Dillon smiled and shook his head at the ridiculousness of the thought. Sometimes he wondered if he was the only one who daydreamed about things that didn't make much sense, or tried to play out unbelievable situations in his mind. When he was a kid, he thought he was weird for envisioning himself as his favorite NBA basketball player, Steve Novak, and pretending to hit the last second shot. It became clear to him as he grew up that everyone who played basketball did that as a kid, and it wasn't very strange at all. However, it seemed a little less normal to Dillon that he continued to set up unrealistic scenarios in his head; after all, he was not 8-years-old anymore.

No one really has to find out about that. What's wrong with daydreaming?

Dillon checked his watch and took a deep breath, realizing that it was almost time to leave for his first class. His nerves suddenly came to life. He realized that he would have to find a seat next to someone in class and introduce himself. He thought about finding a friend to replace Will in his life and knew that he could never do it. He thought about taking notes at the college level and started to have a minor freak-out.

The phone in Dillon's pocket felt heavy, and he contemplated calling his mom, telling her to turn around and take him home. He took another deep breath and bit his lip as he looked at his phone. He remembered his agreement with Martin and knew he couldn't back out now. Putting his phone back in his pocket, Dillon grabbed his backpack.

He checked his schedule again; he had printed himself a copy to help him remember where all his classes would be. It had somehow worked out that all of Dillon's classes were on the same three days of the week. Looking at his watch, he knew it was that time.

Now or never.

He turned the doorknob, took one last deep breath, pulled the door open, and stepped into the hallway. No one was there.

Well, this is nice.

He shut and locked the door and walked down the stairs to leave.

As he walked down the sidewalk to his first class, Dillon started to notice that he was literally the only person on the campus. The place was like a ghost town, minus the spooky buildings and spider webs.

Did Martin start my college classes before everyone else's? This is weird.

As puzzling as it was to look around and see no one, Dillon didn't want to be late for his first class so he decided to disregard the emptiness and continue down the sidewalk.

It was a gorgeous late-summer day, and the sunlight was hot on Dillon's face. As he walked, he started to regret his decision to wear jeans and a polo, but he had figured he would try to make some kind of good impression on his peers. He reached up and felt his hair; he was trying the grungy, It-doesn't-look-like-I-tried-but-it-actually-took-20-minutes look. He wasn't really sure how he felt about the disheveled hairstyle, but it had to be better than anything he'd tried before.

He walked up to the front doors of the business building as he had done with Martin a couple weeks before. He glanced at the bench they had sat on and thought briefly about Martin's charismatic personality and charm. He looked back up at the grey structure in front of him and the glass doors he was just steps from entering. It had been so much less intimidating when he thought he would never step foot inside. Now just looking at it made his stomach do a little twirl.

There was still no one around; the inside of the business building didn't look any more populated than the deserted walk he had just finished. He wondered for a moment if he was here on the wrong day, but he quickly pushed the thought from his mind.

It's impossible to go to college on the wrong day. My mom started counting down the days until my first day of college when I was born.

He glanced up one more time at the business building.

I made it this far…

Dillon stepped inside the first doors and double-checked his schedule. The last thing he wanted to do on his first day of school was walk into the wrong classroom. He had seen movies where it had happened, and he wasn't about to subject himself to that kind of embarrassment.

He checked his watch again, which was now more of a nervous habit than anything. Two minutes until his class started. He took the stairs two at a time, and hustled down the third floor hallway. He made sure to meticulously look at the room numbers, not that it would matter much if he went into the wrong room because all of them were empty.

Dillon arrived outside of room 365 and stopped.

This is it…right?

Before looking inside, he triple-checked his schedule and looked at his watch one more time.

One day to make a decision. My direction will become clear.

He reached for the door handle, and twisted it slowly. As he pulled the door open, he stopped. There were no students inside the room, just one man standing at the front. Dillon was extremely confused to see a very familiar face waiting for him to enter.

Z

Dillon's high school basketball coach, Coach Z, stood towering over the whiteboard at the front of the room. He was a mountain of a man who could intimidate just about anyone. His 6 foot 8 inch frame had made him a powerful basketball player at the University of Wisconsin years earlier. After his four years playing Division One basketball, he joined the Army and served his country until he retired as a Major. Upon retiring from the military, he became a high school English teacher and head basketball coach.

Dillon couldn't think of one student from his high school that would slack off in Coach Z's classes. A meeting in Coach Z's office was about as intimidating as a meeting with the President of the United States. Needless to say, no one wanted to have, "See me after class," written on an assignment.

Although Coach Z rarely smiled himself, he did have an intelligent sense of humor that Dillon appreciated. The problem with his jokes was that students weren't always sure if he was kidding, and they were afraid that they'd be reprimanded if they laughed at the wrong time.

Although he was slightly balding, Coach Z always kept his hair in a perfect military high-and-tight. He was a man who loved precision in every aspect of his life. He expected exceptional writing from his students, and would not settle for half-hearted effort on the basketball court either.

There were definitely people who disliked Coach Z because of his high standards, but Dillon had always had a great relationship with him. Dillon saw early on that people who spoke poorly about Coach Z were people who disliked being held accountable for their actions. Even Dillon's friends on the basketball team might say that Coach Z was always angry and they didn't like it, but Dillon saw the difference between anger and intensity. He would often tell his peers, "You don't have to be angry to be intense. He just wants us to be successful."

Over time, Dillon even started to enjoy going into Coach Z's office and having casual conversations. Dillon would talk to him about the basketball team or books that they had read in class. Despite Coach Z's ability to intimidate, there was a thoughtful aspect to his words that provided an interesting outside perspective on Dillon's views.

But now, seeing Coach Z in his usual polo shirt tightly tucked into khaki pants, Dillon was not sure how to react. He was ready to ask Coach Z what was going on, but Coach Z recognized the confusion on Dillon's face and spoke first.

"How are you, Pal?"

Dillon wasn't sure how to respond. "I'm doing fine. What's going on?"

"Can't your old coach come visit you at college?" Although Coach Z had not removed the stern look from his face, he was clearly joking and Dillon gave a confused smile.

Coach Z continued. "I'm here for you." He didn't say it in the sympathetic way that Dillon had become so accustomed to hearing, but more matter-of-factly. "Come with me." Coach Z led him out of the classroom, down the stairs, and out of the building before he said anything more.

Coach Z looked forward as he walked. "I'm here because I never emphasized the importance of one thing." His voice was firm as it always was.

Dillon tried to keep pace with Coach Z's long strides. "What is it?"

Coach Z disregarded the question as if it hadn't been asked and continued to speak while looking straight ahead, "Everyone in your life makes some kind of impact on the way you are or how you see things. People will influence you positively and negatively, but what you learn from them is just a fraction of what they could and would tell you if the situation was right."

Dillon didn't really understand what this meant, but Coach Z kept talking. "You only see a small portion of the actions of others. You only hear what they say when they're around you, and most of the time, these interactions aren't very blunt. They force you to draw your own conclusions."

While the thought made sense to Dillon, he wasn't very sure where Coach Z was going with this. He waited for Coach Z to speak again as they continued to walk.

"This is why I'm here. I'm here to tell you something. I'm here to talk to you about a lesson that you may or may not have picked up from me over the past four years of high school." Coach Z turned his head and looked Dillon directly in the eyes as he walked past Gesu church. "Even though I'm confident you should know this by now..." Dillon smiled because he thought it was a joke, but quickly removed the smirk when Coach Z remained straight-faced. "Some things need to be said out loud. You may already think you know them, but until you hear them said, in the most blunt way possible, it's hard to make them staples of your life."

Coach Z knew this was a long explanation for why he was here, so he summed it up to help Dillon completely understand, "I'm here to give you one lesson that will help you succeed in college or in life; a lesson that I've never stressed the importance of before. That is why I'm here...that is why we're all here."

Coach Z's words hung in the air for a moment; Dillon wasn't very sure what he meant. "That's why who is all here?"

"You have five classes today, don't you?"

At that moment, Dillon realized what would be happening today.

I'm here to learn all of the lessons I should have learned in high school that will make me successful later on.

While the concept of the day was now clear to Dillon, he was still very skeptical of the idea that he would learn anything or that the day would change his mind about college. He definitely started to feel skeptical about Martin's extravagant promises. He thought back to all of the reasons that he wasn't ready for college, and was ready to defend his position with Coach Z or anyone else that asked. Right on cue, Coach Z's next words seemed to respond to Dillon's thoughts.

"But don't start to think, Dillon, that Martin doesn't have some twists planned for you. He did say you would remember this day for the rest of your life."

Dillon tried to initiate the next portion of the conversation. "So what is the lesson that I'm supposed to learn?"

The question came just as Coach Z led Dillon into the Al McGuire Center, where the Marquette basketball team holds every practice. "That's the thing. I'm not going to tell you unless I know you're open to hearing it. I thought to myself, anyone can give you advice, but unless there is motivation for you to listen to it, the advice is meaningless. So I have a proposition for you."

Dillon didn't know where this was going. "Okay."

"You're going to play one game of 'HORSE'. If you win, you can move forward with your day with any type of attitude you would like. If you lose, you need to keep an open mind all day. You need to listen to all of the lessons that are presented to you, and not jump to any conclusions until the day is over."

Dillon thought about the proposition. Coach Z had played college basketball, but that was many years ago. He knew that Coach Z was not a high level player anymore, and thought about how easy it would be to beat him.

Coach Z continued as he led Dillon down onto the McGuire Center court. "If you agree to this, there's no going back on it. You need to be a man of your word and keep an open mind all day."

This seems easy enough.

"Deal."

As Dillon's hand met Coach Z's to shake on the agreement, another man walked onto the floor from a doorway on the side of the gym.

The man that entered the gym was someone that Dillon immediately recognized, but had only seen on television. He was wearing an old Marquette basketball practice jersey and shorts that went to his knees. He strode slowly onto the court with a basketball in his hand and stopped when he reached Dillon and Coach Z.

Dillon could barely get the words out as he stuttered. "Dwyane Wade?"

Coach Z gave a rare smile. "Oh, Dillon, I forgot to tell you. Your game of 'HORSE' isn't against me. It's against Marquette legend and NBA All-Star, Dwyane Wade. Good thing we shook on it."

Dillon was too awestruck at the thought of playing basketball with Dwyane Wade to argue that the deal was illegitimate.

"How…umm…" Dillon looked toward Coach Z, then back at Dwyane. "Nice to meet you!" The exclamation from Dillon made him feel like a little kid as he reached out an awkward hand to greet the basketball star.

Dwyane smiled, "You too."

There was a moment of silence. Dillon couldn't remove a goofy smile from his face. He wasn't really sure what to say next, but he managed to get out "Uhh…Well, can I shoot first?"

Dwyane laughed and passed him the ball. Dillon realized he was shaking a little bit. He never thought he would be this star struck, but this was the first famous person he had ever met. His first shot bounced hard off the backboard

44

without even hitting the rim. He got his own rebound and threw the ball to his opponent.

The next two minutes couldn't have passed faster. Dwyane hit nine shots in a row, and although Dillon managed to make a few, the game was over before the basketball star had even broken a sweat.

Dwyane walked over to Dillon and shook his hand. "Good game."

Dillon, still in awe of the entire situation, shyly said, "You too."

Coach Z had taken a seat in the first row of the bleachers. Dillon and Dwyane exchanged basketball stories as they walked over and took seats next to him.

When they sat down, Coach Z gave Dillon a look that he knew was asking, "Are you ready to keep an open mind?"

Even though he felt a little cheated, Dillon reluctantly gave a nod. "Alright, Coach, I lost the bet. I'll try to keep an open mind today. So, what's the first lesson?"

Coach Z looked back at Dillon and said, "Don't do stupid stuff."

Dillon's eyebrows wrinkled skeptically, and he glanced up at Coach Z.

"Easy, right?" Coach Z said very seriously.

Dillon felt strange about the simplicity of the lesson. "That's it?"

Coach Z gave a barely visible smirk. "That's it."

There was a small pause as the words lingered in the air before Coach Z continued. "I told you the lessons would be blunt. It's amazing to me how many people do stupid stuff on a regular basis."

When he said this, even Dwyane gave a nod to acknowledge the validity of the statement.

Dillon started to think about all of the celebrities who have everything that they need to live a luxurious life, but do stupid things that put it all at risk.

Coach Z spoke seriously. "You can call it whatever you'd like; some people say, 'be responsible,' other people say, 'take ownership of your actions,' but you've known me long enough to know that I'm not going to sugar-coat the message like that. When people say, 'be responsible,' what does that really mean?" Coach Z shrugged his shoulders. "I don't know what it means. It's vague and has lost it's meaning because people use it too much. It's much easier to think about your actions and ask yourself, 'is this stupid?' Then you need to ask yourself, 'would Coach Z think this is stupid?' If the answer to either of those questions is yes, you need to think strongly about whether you should proceed."

It was strange for Dillon to think about this lesson because Coach Z was right; it was something that he already knew, but it was also something that was never told to him in an honest, straightforward way.

Coach Z interrupted Dillon's thought. "Isn't it baffling to think about how many people would be affected by this lesson if they chose to follow it? Politicians who make unethical decisions, movie stars who overdose on drugs, college students who go to the hospital from drinking too much…All because they do some stupid stuff."

Dillon looked at the ground. "Sometimes it's hard not to." Dillon wasn't trying to be rude, but he found himself thinking about Will.

Would things have been different?

"I agree, Dillon, but many times it's easier to stop yourself from making a bad decision if you recognize that it's not smart. A lot of people act before thinking, and that's when you get into trouble."

Dillon shook his head. "But what if I do the, 'is it stupid' test and still make the wrong decision?"

Coach Z looked Dillon straight in the eyes, which would have caused most of Dillon's high school classmates to cringe. "You cannot always make the right choices, but you can always work to make the choices you *make* the right ones."

Time stopped for a moment. Attending college was a choice that had been heavy on Dillon's mind, and he realized that Coach Z was not going to try to talk him into it. Coach Z just expected Dillon, no matter what decision he made, to work to make it one that would make him happy and lead him in a positive direction.

Coach Z continued seriously. "This may seem small to you, but this is a lesson that can save lives…it could have saved Will's."

This statement hit Dillon hard. Although he had been wondering if things would be different if Coach Z gave this lesson to Will several months ago, he wasn't ready to hear it said out loud. Dillon knew that the decisions Will made that night were not smart, but he didn't want to think that one small decision could have saved Will's life.

Dillon looked back at the floor and before he could think of the best way to respond, Coach Z stood up. "Well, Dillon, I'm not going to overwork you on your first day of college, but I do have one small assignment for you."

Coach Z reached into the back pocket of his khaki pants and pulled out a small piece of paper. It was sharply folded several times and slightly tattered from being in his pocket. As he handed the piece of paper to Dillon, he gave what almost looked like a smile and said, "It's a little wrinkled; you know how unorganized I am."

Dillon returned a small smile, knowing that Coach Z may very well be the most organized man in the world. He looked back down at the ground still a little taken aback by Coach Z's straightforward comments about Will.

Coach Z took two steps toward the door and turned around. "Look, Dillon, you may not like everything you hear today, but it is our job to be completely honest and blunt with you. If there was ever a time to tell it like it is, it's today. Keep your head up, and keep your mind open."

With that, Coach Z turned back around and strode toward the door where Dwyane had walked in.

Dillon managed to say, "Thanks, Coach," as Coach Z turned the door handle.

Coach Z turned back toward Dillon. "Don't mention it." He then ducked beneath the doorframe and the door shut behind him.

Dwyane had been listening intently to Coach Z, but hadn't said much since the game of 'HORSE'. He stood up slowly and continued to face the court. "The guy knows what he's talking about. Don't underestimate how important that lesson can be." With that, he turned toward Dillon, "You remember your way out?"

Dillon nodded as he shook hands with Dwyane and tried to take in how surreal the moment was. Then Dwyane spoke genuinely. "Good luck with everything."

"Thanks."

With that, Dwyane turned and walked out of the gym the way he had come in.

Dillon sat for a moment, thinking about how hard Coach Z's words had hit him. It was hard for him to think that the lesson would make much difference in his life; he had already made up his mind about college, and it didn't help him get over the loss of Will in any way. He was upset that Coach Z would even bring Will up in his "stupid stuff" lesson, but he remembered his agreement to keep an open mind and not get discouraged. It also started to dawn on him that it might have been something that he needed to hear. He thought about some of the "stupid stuff" he and Will had done in high school; some of it was harmless, innocent fun, but that's not what Coach Z was talking about. There were other times that Dillon knew they had not been very responsible.

He looked down at the small piece of paper that Coach Z had given him, unfolded it, and started to read the assignment.

Lesson One
I Will Not Do Stupid Stuff

I will not do stupid stuff. I will do my best to be responsible and avoid any and all types of stupid stuff that cross my mind and my path. I will always take a step back before doing something questionable and analyze the situation with an open mind.

Would my family think this is stupid? My teachers? My coaches? My friends?

I will always ask questions before I act, and not let a lack of knowledge lead me to unfortunate consequences. I realize that my actions are the outcome of my thoughts, and that by thinking clearly, I will avoid making overtly bad decisions.

Realizing that not all decisions are crystal clear, and that I cannot always make the right decisions, I will work hard to make the decisions that I do make the right ones. Once I have come to a conclusion, I will strive to make it the best option I could have chosen.

If I make a bad decision, I will take responsibility for my actions and move forward in the best way possible. I will not pass the buck. My actions are mine alone, and I have no one else to blame for them.

I understand that, although it is seemingly small, the impact this lesson can have on my life is enormous. It could potentially be the difference between life and death.

I will be responsible. I will not do stupid stuff.

Homework:

Make smart decisions every day.

The Podium

Dillon sat for a moment in the bleachers thinking about the note he had just received from Coach Z. He considered the effect that this small decision could have on his life, and although he knew it could keep him from doing anything that he blatantly should not be doing, he wasn't completely convinced that it could change his life.

I already keep myself from doing stupid stuff.

As he was second-guessing the longevity of Coach Z's lesson, Dillon remembered his promise. It started to make sense to Dillon why Coach Z made him agree to keep an open mind through the entire day. Now, because Dillon lost to Dwyane Wade, he could not start to judge the lessons until he received all of them and his final decision about college was the only thing left to think about. He smiled to himself; Coach Z knew what he was doing.

Real smooth, Coach. Real smooth.

It was still hard for Dillon to believe he had just played basketball with an NBA All-Star. He started to daydream about the experience until he found himself staring at a clock in the gym and realized he only had ten minutes to make it to his next class. He stood up and folded the paper that Coach Z had left with him. He pushed the paper into his front pocket and thought of Martin as he walked briskly toward the door.

My direction will become clear.

Walking into the sunshine, he couldn't help but feel lonely. The campus was still completely empty. No cars passed by; no students were walking to classes. Aside from Coach Z and Dwyane Wade, Dillon had seen literally no one. While he initially hated the thought of meeting new people, he now was overwhelmed by the quiet. Dillon took a moment standing in front of the Al McGuire Center.

Where is everyone? This cannot be the way Martin wanted me to feel.

The thought of quitting crossed Dillon's mind, but he had made promises to both Martin and Coach Z. Not only did he have to stay for the entire day, he had to keep an open mind while doing so. Dillon lowered his head and walked quickly to his next classroom.

He got back to the business building with two minutes to spare, and ran up the stairs to the fourth floor. Running the stairs had made Dillon a little out of breath as he took his schedule out of his pocket and made sure he was headed to the right classroom.

Next time I'm taking the elevator.

Curiosity had taken hold of Dillon as he approached the door, which surprisingly made him far less nervous. He took a deep breath, turned the handle, and stepped into the classroom slowly; no one was there. He moved toward the whiteboard and saw a small note on the wooden table at the front of the room. It read:

"Please forgive me for being late. While I am excited to meet with you, my schedule is typically very full, and earlier meetings in my day often compromise my punctuality. Make no mistake that I place a high level of importance on this meeting, but you will have to forgive me and have a seat until I arrive."

Dillon wished there had been a signature on the paper so he'd know whom to expect, but the anonymous note had simply told him to sit and be patient. He wondered if patience had anything to do with the second lesson or if the note simply meant exactly what it said; he didn't have much time to ponder the question as the door opened before he had a chance to sit down.

Dillon didn't know how to respond as a man in a slick grey suit stepped through the doorway; it was a man that Dillon had seen many times in his home-town, but had never had a conversation with.

Mayor Davis.

Anyone from Dillon's hometown would recognize Mayor Davis. He was as close to a celebrity as Dillon's small town had. Mayor Davis was in his forties, but looked as if he were in his early thirties. He had broad shoulders and looked the part of a successful politician. His short silvering hair was gelled casually to the side, and every girl from Dillon's high school had a not-so-secret crush on the man. Dillon had always wondered how extensive Mayor Davis' wardrobe must have been because he always seemed to wear a new suit. Will had always joked that the only differences between Mayor Davis and George Clooney were ten years and several movie parts. There had been speculations recently that Mayor Davis was looking to run for a higher position, but Dillon didn't know enough about politics to keep track.

"Dillon, great to see you," Mayor Davis said with a charismatic smile. He moved toward Dillon to shake his hand, and noticing that Dillon was holding onto the small piece of paper his assistant had left on the table, he added, "I'm glad you got my note."

Mayor Davis had never been a big fan of small talk; he was a man who got to the point and didn't waste many words. He shook Dillon's hand firmly and looked him in the eye as if he were trying to win a vote. Mayor Davis spoke before the handshake even ended. "We're going to take a little walk…"

Dillon nodded, but wished he could sit down. He was already a little tired from the first lesson and all of the stairs he had to climb.

This is way more walking than high school.

Mayor Davis spoke light-heartedly. "I like to walk and talk. It adds a level of attentiveness; I don't want you falling asleep while I tell you the single most important thing about going to college."

Dillon smiled.

If I even go to college.

Although Dillon was very unsure, he didn't want to offend the mayor. "You know I wouldn't fall asleep while you talk."

As the two walked out of the classroom door and down the stairs, Mayor Davis continued. "Dillon, before we get outside, I need to ask you…how is your attention span?"

Dillon was a little confused. "Pretty good, why?"

"There are going to be a lot of distractions during my lesson; I need you to stay completely focused."

Dillon still didn't really understand as they approached the bottom of the stairs.

I haven't seen anyone all day, what could possibly be so distracting?

As Dillon and Mayor Davis turned onto the last set of stairs before the glass front doors, Dillon saw them; hundreds, maybe even thousands, of people were gathered outside the business building, cheering and waiting for the two to come outside.

How did they get out here so fast?

The people had formed in two rows that would allow the two of them to walk through the middle. He noticed that at the end of the long walkway formed by the people was a stage with a microphone and a podium. A small distance behind the podium was a beautiful pathway leading up to the Joan of Arc Chapel. Dillon couldn't help but think about how amazing the backdrop was with all of the colorful flowers leading up to the old chapel. Next to the podium in the distance, stood Martin, waiting for Mayor Davis and Dillon to proceed through the crowd.

Martin had the same cheerful smile that Dillon remembered vividly. His purple suit-coat and green bow tie seemed just as ridiculous today as they did the first time Dillon saw them. Martin had the same beige pants and brown shoes on, but this time he was sporting a light brown top hat that tilted slightly to the right.

Do I have to speak in front of all these people?

Dillon realized he wasn't breathing and quickly took a breath. He managed to speak quietly. "What's going on?"

"Just a small gathering. Something like a parade. I had a major speech scheduled for today; I figured, why not give it here?"

Both Dillon and Mayor Davis stopped at the bottom of the stairs and looked out the doors as everyone continued to cheer. Dillon wasn't prepared for this at all; he was confused as the number of people outside looked like the entire population of his hometown, but he didn't recognize anyone. So many questions were racing through his head.

Who are all these people?

Is this part of the lesson?

Mayor Davis continued, "As I explained in the note earlier, my time is very limited, but I promise you that I have put a considerable amount of time into the formulation of this lesson. What I'd like to talk to you about is relevant to your life, and very practical in your decision-making process. However, I need to give you this lesson between here and that podium as we walk slowly and wave to the crowd. Can you stay focused?"

Dillon had always gotten a little nervous in front of crowds, but he was relieved that Mayor Davis wasn't making him stand at the podium and address the people.

"Yeah, I can stay focused."

"That's great news. Put on a smile, it's go time!"

Mayor Davis flung the door open and threw up his hand in an emphatic wave to the crowd. Dillon moved behind Mayor Davis, trying hard not to look nervous.

I should have worn something nicer.

As they walked forward through the middle of the cheering crowd, Mayor Davis started his lesson. "Dillon, I didn't always want to be in politics," he said with a smile as he continued to wave to the crowd. "Early on, I thought a business career was going to be the best fit for me. Even when I started pursuing politics, I wasn't always convinced that it was what I would do for the rest of my life."

Dillon felt a little strange hearing this; the mayor had always seemed incredibly happy with his job.

The mayor didn't hesitate. His words were smooth as if all of his responses had been rehearsed. "I got to a pivotal point where I either had to go one direction or the other, just like you."

"Why did you choose politics?"

Mayor Davis smiled, this time only at Dillon. "Honestly, Dillon, I don't know."

There was a small pause before Mayor Davis continued. "That's the lesson, Dillon. You still focused?"

Dillon nodded.

"Take action. You can't always make the right decision; Coach Z told you that in lesson one, but it is a powerful message. If I hadn't committed to becoming the best politician I could be, I would have always been questioning whether it was the right choice. Instead of focusing on these negative thoughts, it was important that I made up my mind, then devoted my time and energy to making it work in my favor. Once a decision is made, the only direction you can move is forward."

Dillon looked back toward the business building. The crowd had gotten considerably more quiet, but they were still happy to wave and cheer as Mayor Davis passed.

Halfway to the podium.

Even with all the people around, Mayor Davis was not distracted. "Alright, Dillon, critical thinking time; I have a question for you."

"Alright."

"If there are three people sitting on a park bench and one of them decides to walk away, how many people are left on the bench?"

Dillon was taken aback by how easy this question seemed. "There are two people left on the bench."

Mayor Davis' eyes narrowed on Dillon, a small smirk on his face. "No, Dillon. There are still three people sitting on the park bench. I said that one person decided to walk away; deciding to walk away and actually walking away are two very different things."

Dillon felt a little tricked, but nodded as Mayor Davis continued.

"I can DECIDE to do just about anything. I can decide to go to college; I can decide to become a politician, but until I take action to make these things happen, I really haven't done anything."

Mayor Davis made sure his point was clear. "Most people will give up on an idea before even getting started. They will get stuck thinking about all the ways it will fail, or they will try to grasp all the aspects before moving forward toward the goal. The truth is, you're never going to understand every outcome of a decision before you make it. The important part is that you take action. Forget about all the limitations, know that every decision comes with a level of uncertainty, and jump in. Before you take action, you really haven't done anything."

A nervous, unsure look crossed Dillon's face and he looked toward the ground.

"What if I fail?"

A wry smile crossed the mayor's face and, even though a crowd surrounded them, Dillon felt like he was the only one there.

"Dillon, everyone fails. But the people who truly succeed are the ones who don't let the fear of failure keep them from trying."

"Most people will fail once or twice, then give up because they think these failures mean that THEY are failures. Nothing could be further from the truth. The only way someone becomes a failure is if they stop failing; this means they've stopped trying."

Mayor Davis paused for a moment.

Almost to the podium.

"Dillon, don't get me wrong, the key to success is not doing things more times than others or taking random action toward things you are not passionate about. It's not about buying more lottery tickets than the next guy. The key to success is committing to taking action toward the best decision available to you at the time. If you continue to take concentrated action, you will not fail."

Up until this point, Dillon had only listened to the mayor, but he was starting to feel uneasy about applying this lesson to his own life.

What type of actions should I choose to pursue?

"What if the action that I take is to not go to college?"

"Take action in a different direction."

Dillon started to realize that this lesson was not just about college; Mayor Davis was giving Dillon a lesson to apply to any situation in his life. Dillon noticed that they were now standing by the stage to the right of the podium, and Mayor Davis took the moment to finish his lesson.

"No matter what you choose, college, no college, businessman, politician, my only hope is that you use your time and energy to commit to your decision, always move forward, take action, and make your decision work out."

With that, Mayor Davis glanced over Dillon's shoulder where Martin was leaning against the stage flipping a quarter and whistling. "Well, Dillon, looks like my time with you is up; I'll leave you with Martin." Mayor Davis reached into his suit pocket and took out a small piece of paper. As the mayor buttoned his coat, he winked at Dillon. "You're a bright kid. I wish you only the best."

Mayor Davis handed Dillon the small piece of paper, and gave him an empowering nod. Before Dillon could say, "Thank you," Mayor Davis had walked up the stairs onto the stage and taken his place at the podium.

The speech began, "Hello, everyone! Thank you for coming to support me in my nomination for United States Congress!"

Dillon was not surprised at all to hear the reason for the Mayor's speech. He glanced down at the paper, then over at Martin. He was still flipping a quarter. In his other hand he held a cane that he clearly did not need. Martin looked up, put the quarter in a pocket in his purple jacket, and gave Dillon a nod. "Let's get out of here."

Dillon kept the paper folded in his hand as Martin led him through the light brick pathway that was surrounded by beautiful flowers in front of the Joan of Arc Chapel. Dillon took the time to think about everything Mayor Davis had said during the walk they had taken through the crowd.

Martin walked Dillon around the vine-covered side of the building and stopped to sit on a bench behind the chapel; although Dillon could still faintly hear Mayor Davis' voice over the microphone, he could no longer see the crowd, and felt a small sense of relief to be able to sit down and quietly read the note Mayor Davis had left him. Dillon's phone vibrated and made a noise in his pocket, but he ignored it, and with Martin sitting next to him, unfolded the paper.

Lesson Two
I Will Take Action

I will take action. I realize that I cannot always make the right decisions, but I can always work to make my decisions the right ones. I will not spend my life looking back and wondering how things could have been different. I will move forward with my decisions, and commit time and energy to ensure a positive result.

I will understand the difference between deciding to do something and actually doing it. I will not be limited by uncertainty or the thought of failure. Every decision involves risk, but I will not let the fear of being unsuccessful keep me from taking action and moving forward toward my goal.

Above all, I will never stop taking action. I will never quit. I will not let my failures define who I am. Rather, I will learn from every failure and use that new knowledge to take action again. Giving up will never be an option. I will continue to take action until I have realized the success I envisioned.

I will be successful. I will take action.

Homework:

Take action every day.

Reaffirmation

When Dillon had finished reading, he looked up. For some reason, Dillon started to feel upset. He started to relive the feelings he had so often felt after Will had passed away. Even with the lessons that he had been given thus far on his "special day," he didn't feel like he was growing or getting anywhere; he still didn't want to attend college after his first day, and he still didn't feel like he could completely let go of Will. He sat motionless with the piece of paper in his hand as these negative thoughts started to control every aspect of his mind.

When will my direction become clear?

It bothered Dillon that Mayor Davis had not mentioned Will. Dillon knew he could have taken action to keep Will from attending the party that night.

He probably wouldn't have listened to me.

Dillon knew it would have been a difficult thing for Mayor Davis to bring up, and an even more difficult thing for Dillon to hear.

On second thought, maybe it's good Mayor Davis didn't say anything.

Dillon thought briefly about giving up. Although he understood the relevance of the first two lessons, nothing he had experienced thus far was as exciting or memorable as Martin had said it would be. With the negative thoughts he had been having, Dillon couldn't help but feel a little unimpressed. Sure, he saw how the first two lessons could have a large impact on anyone's life, but at this point, he didn't really care.

No lesson can replace the fact that Will is gone, and that I'm not ready for college.

Dillon caught himself staring at the ground, and started to feel like he was letting down Coach Z.

I promised to keep an open mind; I'm not doing a very good job right now.

He looked up to scan his surroundings, and his eyes lit up as he took in the extravagance of the scenery. The bright red and yellow flowers surrounding the old building were in full bloom, and although the sun was shining brightly, several larger trees that surrounded the chapel shaded the bench that he and Martin sat on. Dillon realized that he had never seen this part of campus before, and wondered why it took him so long to see how beautiful it was. The answer was pretty clear to him.

It's because I've been looking at the ground feeling sorry for myself.

Dillon felt his attitude shift in that moment. It was as if all of his doubts faded into the air. His negative energy was just...gone. In one instant, he went from close-to-quitting, to content and excited for the rest of the day. He wasn't sure what brought on this quick turnaround, but whatever it was, he wasn't going to fight it.

With his newfound dedication to the day, Dillon glanced at Martin who was looking up at a squirrel jumping between branches. As if Martin felt Dillon's eyes move toward him, he broke the silence.

"You know what's interesting to me?"

"What?"

"Squirrels are so small, but can jump a distance of up to 20 feet, and they rarely fall."

Martin's off-topic comment made Dillon shake his head with a smile, and Martin continued.

"It's pretty crazy. They can fall up to 100 feet without being injured because they use their tails like a parachute! It's true. Look it up."

Dillon couldn't help but let out a laugh now. "How do you know so much about squirrels?"

Martin scrunched his eyebrows quizzically. "You know, Dillon...I'm not sure." Then Martin stood up quickly, "Walk with me, my boy!"

Dillon folded the small piece of paper from Mayor Davis and placed it in his pocket next to the first lesson he received.

"Second lesson completed!" Martin said as he turned to walk back to the front of the chapel. Martin's pace had not slowed a bit since Dillon's first meeting with him. Dillon followed, being sure to notice the flowers and plants that filled the walkway. As Martin and Dillon moved toward where Mayor Davis had left them, Dillon looked up and froze.

"Where did everyone go?"

Dillon and Martin stood overlooking the large space that, just moments before, had been filled with a cheering crowd. Mayor Davis was nowhere in sight. The podium had already been taken down. The Marquette campus was, once again, completely deserted.

A million questions whizzed through Dillon's mind.

How did everyone leave so fast?

Was his speech really that short?

Did I really not hear everyone leaving?

Martin did not seem to be fazed. "Follow me, my boy." Dillon had almost forgotten how quickly Martin thinks, but he remembered as Martin began to speak.

"You've obviously noticed that this will not be an ordinary day for you; if you hadn't noticed, I just ruined the surprise. But I thought I would stop by to reemphasize something as you continue forward in your day."

There was a short pause. Dillon was still extremely confused.

Could they really have cleared this area already?

Dillon felt as though his confusion somehow cut off Martin's words, but in looking back at Martin realized he had only stopped speaking to look at a small bird that had landed ten feet in front of them. The small bird flew away as they approached it. Dillon smiled, thinking that Martin must either have a thing for animals or some sort of attention problem. But he couldn't get over how empty the area was after being filled moments earlier. Martin snapped back into the conversation.

"Yes, I needed to come by to reemphasize something. While this was not the primary lesson of your first course, it was an important aspect that needs to be honored."

Martin continued swiftly, but with his typical charming demeanor. "You must keep an open mind through the entire day. While all of the lessons today are meant to be straightforward, in some instances, you will not understand the answers to 'how' or 'why' things are happening." Martin and Dillon continued to walk swiftly toward the next classroom on Dillon's schedule. "Even the statement I've just made probably does not make complete sense to you, but when the situation arises, you must commit to staying present and listening no matter how strange the situation seems."

Dillon knew that Martin was answering all of the questions he had just been wondering about with a pretty obvious, "Don't ask."

While Dillon somewhat understood what Martin was telling him, his curiosity was getting the best of him. "So how did all these people get out of sight so quickly and quietly?"

Martin smiled at him. "Did I just hear you say, 'how'? Remember, you agreed to keep an open mind no matter what happens. Breaking that promise would be like breaking an expensive vase in your grandparents house when you were ten; funny how you never forget about something like that." Martin looked up as if he were remembering a disturbing event in his past, then continued.

"The important part is not HOW these people left, but the fact that they are gone. If you start to think about how the events of this day are taking place, you will lose sight of the important lessons that are being taught. Let me worry about how things happen."

Dillon nodded, not truly understanding what Martin was talking about. "So, you're saying that no matter what happens, I should just roll with the situation?"

"Precisely! Accept that there are things you will not understand, and move forward as if those things are not important."

"Okay. I'll do my best." Dillon thought for a moment. "Is this one of my lessons?"

Martin gave a sarcastic laugh. "Ha! I'm no professor. This is an unofficial lesson. One you only have to remember for today."

Dillon nodded and checked his watch. "Alright, Martin. I'll keep an open mind, and I'll try not to question the parts that don't make sense to me."

"That's the spirit!"

Dillon and Martin were nearing the doors of a building called Lalumiere Hall, which Dillon thought was one of the strangest looking buildings on Marquette's campus. It was symmetrically square and painted white, but the front was covered in shapes that made it look like a large honeycomb. Within some of the shapes were windows that looked much darker in contrast to the pure white that was the rest of the building.

Martin interrupted the silence. "I'll let you get to your next class. You're moving along splendidly. Keep an open mind; three classes to go."

With a smile and a tip of his top hat with the cane he hadn't been using, Martin turned and strode away quickly as if he had something else urgent to attend to. Dillon smiled and shook his head knowing that Martin had no other urgent engagements, but simply treated every task as if it were the most important thing he could set his mind to.

Dillon turned and looked up at the outside of the honeycomb-like structure. He couldn't help but feel intimidated. This was a building he hadn't been in before, and he was headed to see a mysterious professor whom he was sure he would recognize. As had become habit on his first day, he got his schedule out of his pocket and checked the classroom number one more time. Then, looking up at the building once more, he exhaled and walked to the front door.

Upon entering, Dillon realized his classroom was closer to the doors than he had previously thought.

And here I was worried about being late.

He walked toward the room and stood in front of the closed door. Reaching for the handle, Dillon jumped as he heard a woman's voice yell, "ATTENTION!" The shout sounded like a military officer was running an exercise in the room. Taking a step back, he waited for a moment before the voice broke the silence with another martial call, "STAND AT, EASE!" He did not recognize the voice and started to get nervous about what this lesson might hold. He strongly started to reconsider entering this room.

I don't want to get yelled at by someone in the military!

As he looked left and right thinking about sneaking back outside, another yell came from inside the room, "ARE YOU THINKING OF QUITTING!? WE NEVER QUIT!" Beads of sweat started to drip down Dillon's forehead.

Was this woman just talking to me? Does she know I'm out here?

Dillon needed a moment to think the situation over so he crouched with his back against the closed classroom door. Another bellow from inside seemed to demand that Dillon make a choice. "YOU'RE ALL IN OR YOU'RE ALL OUT!

WHAT'S IT GOING TO BE?" There was a moment of silence that allowed Dillon to start to organize his thoughts.

The person inside has to be someone here for me, right? Everything is going to be fine...right?

Although Dillon didn't think Martin would find it beneficial to bring someone in to shout at him, he was still sitting on the floor with his back against the door. Part of him was waiting for another command or for Martin to come whistling through the front doors; he was waiting for anything but the silence that he was currently sitting in.

Okay, I'll get up in five seconds and go into this room. Keep an open mind, Dillon. Keep an open mind.

Dillon couldn't help but breathe hard as he sat slumped against the door.

Five.

As soon as he started the countdown, Dillon realized just how nervous he was to enter this room.

Four.

He hadn't made any movement to stand up or reach for the door handle, but he knew the countdown had to continue.

Three.

Dillon closed his eyes and felt a bead of sweat drip down his cheek.

Two.

Just as Dillon moved to slide his body up the middle of the door, someone yanked it open from the inside, and Dillon fell hard into the classroom. As he looked up into familiar eyes, he had a million more questions to ask.

War Stories

Dillon's grandmother stood over him with a large assault rifle in her hands. The sight took Dillon aback. She was wearing an old, faded military uniform; it was dark green with a white undershirt. Dillon wasn't sure if he should be comforted to see his grandmother or fearful because of the way she was dressed and the weapon she was holding. She had gray hair that was tucked back into a tight bun behind her head. Her face was wrinkled and weathered, but her eyes stayed youthful. Her hands were tightly wrapped around the weapon in her hands, which was strange for Dillon to see as he had only seen those hands weak with arthritis. Dillon stayed on the ground for a moment, hoping she would break the silence. It wasn't long before she did.

"Hello, Dillon." She said calmly in the gentle voice that Dillon was accustomed to hearing from his grandmother. "Forgive me if I startled you. I was just reminiscing about my time in the service." She reached out her hand and pulled Dillon up off of the ground.

That is the weirdest way I've ever heard anyone reminisce.

Dillon looked to the front of the room where his grandmother had moved several desks to clear a small space.

Noticing him looking curiously at the area, Dillon's grandmother spoke.

"You know, when I was in the service, they didn't allow women to hold a rifle like this."

She's had arthritis for years! How does she have the strength to hold on to a weapon that size?

Dillon's grandmother interrupted his thought. "Do you want to hold it?"

"No, thanks."

This is the strangest situation I've ever been in.

Dillon's grandmother laughed. "Suit yourself; that's not why I'm here." She lowered the weapon and skillfully began taking the whole thing apart. "You know, Dillon, there's a lot about me that you don't know. There are things that I couldn't tell you when you were little; you wouldn't have understood."

Her hands moved swiftly as she disassembled the entire weapon. When she was finished she glanced down at it. "What an amazing rifle. We didn't have these when I was in the Army."

"Grandma, what about your arthritis?" The words came out of Dillon's mouth quickly, and afterword he felt bad that he asked.

"I put that aside for today." She smiled slyly.

That doesn't make sense.

"Anyway, Dillon, you're here to learn a lesson from me."

Dillon decided to set his confusion aside and listen to his grandmother, mostly because of his conversation with Martin about keeping an open mind. Dillon started to think about what Martin was doing at that very moment.

Probably staring in wonder at a flock of geese overhead.

He smiled at the thought, but his grandmother brought him back to the present.

"Since we have a moment, I'd like to tell you a couple stories. You may not believe it, but I've seen quite a bit in my lifetime. Come take a seat."

Dillon walked with her and sat in a desk toward the front of the room. He felt like he was about to get lectured, which he wasn't exactly excited about. To Dillon's surprise, his grandmother started with a question.

"Do you know much about war, Dillon?"

"Not really, I learned about the history of some wars in school." Dillon still was not sure what to think about the scenario in front of him.

Dillon's grandmother nodded as if she had anticipated his answer. "I think that most people your age would say the same. I think you'll find that there is a large difference between your history classes and the lesson I will share with you today."

She looked toward the window and thought for a moment before pressing on. "Your history classes will tell you about events; they will tell you about important leaders, the conflicts that arose, and dates to remember. Your history classes will take most of the emotion out of it. They will not talk to you about how the soldiers felt, on an individual level, while all of this was happening."

She paused for a moment as if she was thinking back. "Being involved in a war is difficult, but you know that already. You've seen action movies, and you know the physical struggles that soldiers go through. What those movies do not portray is the mental toughness that is associated with being a soldier."

Dillon noticed how strategic her pauses were; he was getting more comfortable sitting next to her as he waited for her to keep talking. He noticed youthfulness in her demeanor. He started to picture her as a young woman serving in the military. Her wrinkles faded away, and her hair became a darker brown instead of the gray he was accustomed to seeing. It was surprisingly easy for Dillon to picture; so much so that the woman talking in front of him did not seem like an old woman anymore at all, but a young version of his grandmother.

She continued. "The hardest part for me was never the physical circumstances, but the way those physical difficulties created mental challenges that my squad had to overcome every day. There were times as a military nurse when I would spend 48 hours straight in the hospital. These types of challenges were normal, and we just had to push through and do the best we could. The funny thing is, there was never one moment that I actually wanted to be a military nurse."

The statement didn't make much sense to Dillon, but his grandmother continued.

"I'd hear stories about what was going on in the field, but as a woman, I was never allowed to hold a rifle. Women were not given the opportunity to fight for their country; that was a job for men. Isn't it amazing how much the world has changed?"

I wonder what her lesson actually is.

As if reading Dillon's mind, his grandmother stated, "Unwavering persistence will absolutely change your life."

"Before I continue, I need you to recognize that I purposely used the example of war and the everyday struggles that we needed to overcome while it was happening. I did this because everyone has battles that they wage on a daily basis, and many of them are internal; things that we do not share with everyone who knows us. Everyone has aspects of their life story that they only share with their family or closest friends, and many people have things that they hold in and do not share at all. There are battles that all of us face daily with the potential to ruin our lives if we let them take complete control. The bright side of all of this is that we all have the opportunity to persevere."

Dillon thought about how little he actually talked about Will to those close to him. Losing his best friend was definitely an internal battle he had been fighting for some time.

His grandmother moved forward with her lesson. "There are little things that take just a small amount of extra effort to combat mentally. Staying up all night to write a paper is something most college students do at one point or another, and it would be easy to get frustrated. But it's a mental choice to push through the physical difficulty of the situation and get the job done."

Dillon continued to think about how difficult it had been for him to overcome Will's death.

What mental choice could I have made to make that situation better? Will was my best friend.

"And sometimes, Dillon, it is much harder to be mentally tough. I told you that I didn't want to be a nurse, and that is true, but I truly had a desire to serve our country. That is where persistence comes in. I decided that I would do my best to persevere in the role that I was given while also fighting for more rights as a woman. I wanted to hold that rifle more than anyone. I was even reprimanded once for picking up the weapon of a fallen soldier to protect myself in the field."

Dillon's grandmother gave a reminiscent look before continuing, "I never got the chance during my time in the military to fight alongside men as an equal, but that's not the point. The point is, I stayed determined to overcome my surroundings and in doing so, I helped pave the way for millions of women who want nothing more than to serve their country in combat. Having unwavering persistence is a choice that has lasting effects."

The gleam in Dillon's grandmother's now-young eyes seemed to fade slightly as her demeanor became more serious. "Sometimes a situation can drastically change your life…"

Dillon's grandmother looked Dillon directly in the eyes, and Dillon knew she was talking about the loss of Will.

"Never give up. Strive to find your mental stability. You can grieve; it's necessary. But don't let situations in your life define who you are."

Dillon started feeling frustrated with the lesson. He wasn't ready to think about Will. He knew he hadn't done a good job of being mentally persistent during this difficult time, but he also felt that his struggles justified how he was feeling and acting.

No one else had to go through what I went through.

He spoke up, but in almost a whisper. "It's harder than you think to persevere, Grandma."

Dillon's grandmother smiled calmly. "You may not believe it, but I know what you're talking about. My decision to join the Army also led me to some of the hardest moments in my life." Dillon could see his grandmother's eyes start to glisten as small tears began to build. "We have more in common than you think, Dillon. When I was twenty years old, I lost my best friend. She was a nurse alongside me in the Army. We had both run to aid an injured soldier." Dillon's grandmother took a deep breath and fought to hold in a tear. "I still remember the mist that seemed to be constantly surrounding us on that day. The mud on the ground was wet and clung to anything it touched. My friend and I knelt on the ground and began evaluating the injury. The trees that surrounded us were tall and made it difficult to see anything...or anyone around us." A tear began to slide down her cheek and she quickly wiped it away. "There were gunshots constantly ringing out, but we did not let them distract us. I turned to my medical kit and took a moment to get the materials I needed...and when I turned back around..." Dillon's grandmother went silent for a moment. "My friend was on the ground next to the soldier. It's a sight I'll never forget." She wiped another tear from her eye and took a moment before continuing.

"As you can see, it is still not easy for me to talk about. I can never pretend that it didn't happen, but *time* is a beautiful thing in that it will heal your heart if you choose to be persistent."

Dillon nodded and kept eye contact with his grandmother, "What happened when you chose to be persistent?"

"I met your grandfather." She smiled through teary eyes. "We started an amazing life together."

Dillon had never known any of this about his grandmother, and he felt like he could connect with her much better than he ever imagined he would.

In a much lighter tone, Dillon's grandmother added, "Persistence isn't just about taking care of yourself mentally and pushing forward through difficult times, though. It applies to just about every area of your life. Think about some of the things that you have given up on in your life."

Both Dillon and his grandmother knew there were more than a few.

Playing trombone, my paper route, participating in track...

She continued, "It is okay to let certain things fall by the wayside. That's life. You decide what is important to you and what is not. But once you know what those important things within your life are, don't ever give up on them."

In a sympathetic tone, Dillon's grandmother continued. "I'm not telling you this lesson is easy. I can think of so many times that I took steps backward when I could have been persistent and moved forward; it happens. But if you can learn anything from me, just remember that unwavering persistence always pays off. Realizing this one small thing can have an amazing effect on your life."

Leaning back in his chair, Dillon started to realize how exhausted he was. This day was nothing like what he thought it would be. The lessons started to form a concise list in Dillon's head.

Don't do stupid stuff.
Take action.

73

Have unwavering persistence.

All of the lessons started to seem far away as he brought himself back to the memory of sitting with Will in the principal's office.

I wonder what Will would want me to do.

Dillon's grandmother smiled, "You've had a lot thrown at you today. I think you need a little time with your own thoughts. And I need a little more time with my weapon." She winked at Dillon with a smirk. She stood up and walked Dillon toward the door. Grabbing the handle, she winced from her arthritis pain. After talking to what seemed like a young version of his grandmother throughout the lesson, Dillon looked up at her to see his old grandmother again; the wrinkles and grey hair appearing once again to Dillon as if her entire aging process took place in the walk from the front of the room to the door. With her hand on the handle, Dillon's grandmother whispered, "If you ever need anything, you know where to find me."

"Thanks, Grandma."

Dillon's grandmother took a small piece of paper from her faded uniform and raised her hand to give it to Dillon. He noticed a small shake in her hand as he took the paper. Dillon gave his grandmother a hug then turned and left the room.

When the door shut behind him, Dillon took a deep breath.

Alright...persistence.

He could feel his heart beating, but not nervously like before entering the room with his grandmother. His heart was beating slowly and heavily. Dillon felt his throat start to close up. He started to feel the lessons of the day digging into his emotions and small tears started to well in his eyes. He knew the lessons could be utilized by anyone, but he felt like they were all tailored to his immediate struggles. He started getting more choked up thinking about all of the people who came to teach him not only about getting by in college, but about living the best life he possibly could. Their presence showed a higher level of care for his well-being than he had felt in a long time.

Breathing heavily and holding back tears, Dillon pushed open the front doors of Lalumiere. There was no one around to tell him not to cry, but Dillon fought hard to keep tears from sliding down his face. He slowly walked to a nearby bench and took a seat.

After three deep breaths, Dillon looked down at the folded piece of paper in his hands. He ran his fingers over the crease, then delicately grabbed the lower edge and opened it.

Lesson Three
I Will Have Unwavering Persistence

I am a person of unwavering persistence. I do not let unfortunate situations in my life defeat me or define who I will become. Only I can define who I become.

I will push forward and work to be mentally strong. I understand that it is okay to get upset or grieve at times because these are natural human emotions, but I will not let these emotions control my thoughts and actions. I will do what is necessary to persevere and find a place where I can, once again, be happy and healthy.

I will decide what is important to me and will promise myself that I will never give up in those areas.

Making the decision to have unwavering persistence will not always be easy. I know that there will be times when giving up will seem easier, but I also know that the easy decision is not always the right decision. I will be confident that my persistence will pay off.

I will have unwavering persistence.

Homework:

Make the decision every day to persist through even the most difficult of times.

Counsel

The sun was high in the sky and the campus still deserted. Though the emptiness of campus had become normal for Dillon, he really didn't want to be alone anymore. Dillon walked briskly toward his next class.

Maybe I'm allowed to be early.

Coming to terms with the lessons he had been given thus far had brought up a lot of emotions that Dillon wasn't exactly sure how to deal with. All of the lessons he had received did not necessarily convince him that college was the right choice for him, but they did make him think about his life more than he had in a long time. It seemed that Coach Z, Mayor Davis, and his grandmother all knew exactly how to get Dillon thinking about what it takes to be successful, no matter what direction he would choose. Dillon was still surprised at how simple and straightforward all of the lessons seemed.

So simple to remember, but so hard to do sometimes.

As Dillon opened the doors once again to the business building, he thought about Will; he thought about how he pushed everyone away after Will was gone. He started to tear up as he remembered slowly deciding that college was not right for him.

Was that just my way of giving up? Of not persevering?

Dillon realized that college would be a different, new experience in his life, but until this point, he didn't view not attending college as "giving up" or lacking the ability to persevere.

That's exactly what it is. I haven't been persistent at all. I let my situation take complete control of my decisions, just as my grandma said.

Dillon wanted so badly to stay positive and hold in his emotions, but realizing that he was not doing a very good job at any of the lessons was too much for him. In every category, he felt he could have done something differently, or could have influenced someone else to do something differently, and it would have changed everything. He started to feel the tears coming and there was no way to hold them back.

What direction do I move in from here?

Making his way up the stairs, tears streamed down his face. He felt like he should not enter his next classroom while crying, but at this point, he didn't have much of an option, and quite frankly, he didn't really care.

They might as well see how I'm really feeling.

Like he had done before every lesson, Dillon double-checked his schedule. He felt the pulsing vibration of his phone ringing in his pocket; he ignored it and took a breath. He stood outside the room in an attempt to gather himself, but after a brief moment, decided it was no use; he turned the knob and pushed the door open.

In the front of the classroom sat his high school guidance counselor, Mr. Rice. Seeing Mr. Rice brought Dillon a rush of emotions. If there was one person who knew close to everything about Dillon, it was Mr. Rice. The man was always around when Dillon needed him and was a constant voice of support and affirmation for Dillon.

The majority of times Dillon met with Mr. Rice, it was because he was sent there to discuss his friendship with Will. There were several times when teachers within the school expressed concern about Will's influence on him. Of course, he didn't really mind. Mr. Rice always made the conversation casual and spent most of the time asking the right questions and listening to Dillon.

With Mr. Rice waiting at the front of his fourth lesson, Dillon realized that he never really found out too much about him.

I'm sure I will hear his story today.

Mr. Rice stood up, and Dillon felt awkward realizing that he was still standing in the doorway. He brushed the last of a tear off of his face and moved toward the front of the room. Mr. Rice stood silently and waited.

Mr. Rice was a shorter man. He was not overweight, but he definitely did not look like he had ever been an athlete. He always wore a gray tweed jacket with elbow patches sewn on, and his round glasses complimented his balding, round head well. Dillon always wondered if other guidance counselors got jealous of Mr. Rice, clearly not because of his looks, but because students always walked directly past their doors to meet with Mr. Rice. He was always the favorite counselor, which was interesting to Dillon because he had never known Mr. Rice to be very outgoing or outspoken.

Dillon was fairly confident that Mr. Rice was a very intelligent person, but it was hard to tell because he rarely told stories about himself or his past. His focus was always on the people he was speaking with.

Dillon felt a little ashamed that he had visibly been crying, but he decided to bashfully break the silence.

"Hey, Mr. Rice."

Mr. Rice looked back with compassion in his eyes. Dillon had never seen Mr. Rice overly emotional in either direction; he was the definition of even-keel.

"Hey Dillon." There was a short pause behind his greeting. Mr. Rice always spoke slowly and calmly. "I heard you've had a long day."

At that moment, Dillon opened up as if he hadn't spoken to anyone in years. The words were flushing out of him before he could even think them over.

"I'm not a quitter, Mr. Rice. I've never been a quitter. It's just, everything in my life has been changing, and I don't know how to handle it all. What if I can't excel in college? What if I don't fit in with the people here?"

The words kept flowing quickly as several tears started to run down Dillon's face. "I know that I did well in high school, and that I should do my best to move on now that Will's gone; I just think about leaving my family and my hometown, and I get…scared."

Dillon paused, thinking about the word. He hadn't actually admitted even to himself that he was scared for the future. It sounded foreign that he would say something that would make him so vulnerable. He instinctively looked down at the ground, feeling embarrassed for his emotional rant; he tried to hold back the tears that were left in his eyes, but he wasn't doing a very good job.

"Mr. Rice, I don't mean to have a breakdown or let you see me like this. It's just been a really long day."

Mr. Rice had been patiently nodding along while he listened. He now asked a question in a slow and compassionate tone. "Have you learned anything new?"

"The lessons I've gotten have all been things that I already know, and I just don't do a very good job at them. I knew that going to that party was a stupid idea, but I didn't try to stop Will. I guess I just thought he wouldn't listen to me. I've taken action, but I constantly think about failing, and that keeps me from trying new things. And when it comes to being persistent, well, I don't think I can make much of an argument that I've done a good job. So I guess, more than anything, I learned that getting better at living these small lessons would make a difference in my life."

When Dillon finished, he took a moment to gather himself and began to realize that he had been the only one contributing to this conversation.

Every other lesson involved a lot of listening. Now my counselor is the one listening.

Wondering when Mr. Rice was going to get to his lesson, Dillon tried to shift the focus away from himself.

Wiping away a tear, he spoke up. "Mr. Rice, I don't mean to be rude, but it seems like we're spending a lot of time talking about me. Shouldn't we be getting to your lesson?"

Mr. Rice answered calmly. "Before we do, I just want to make sure that you are okay." He looked at Dillon as if it was a question.

"Yeah. I think there has just been a lot to think about lately."

"Well, remember that if you need anything, my phone is always on and my door is always open."

Dillon gave an appreciative smile. "Thanks. So what is this lesson?"

Mr. Rice gave a small smile before he started. "This lesson is all about what just took place."

Dillon didn't understand the comment at all, but his counselor continued calmly.

"It is about listening when someone needs an ear, or helping when someone needs a hand. My lesson is to commit to serving others with a selfless heart."

There was a pause as if Mr. Rice felt no explanation was necessary. Dillon thought for a moment. "Is that why you became a counselor?"

"It is definitely part of the reason. I needed to find for myself a profession where I could wake up every day excited about what I do. I struggled for a long time thinking about what that may be, and it all came to me when I was on a service trip to El Salvador."

A flashback of numerous pictures in his counselor's office moved through Dillon's mind. He remembered pictures of tattered villages and children in poverty around the desk or hanging on the wall, but he never asked about them.

Probably because I was so focused on myself.

"I was tutoring a high school-aged boy one day. Everything was going fine, until the boy snapped. He threw down his pencil and refused to do any more work. I could tell there was something seriously troubling the boy so I put the lesson on hold, and we talked about his life for the next half hour."

"You speak Spanish?"

"Yes. I decided to learn after my first service trip in middle school. Hard to picture me that young, huh?"

Dillon smiled at the joke, but it actually was pretty difficult to picture.

"The boy told me about his rough upbringing, his daily struggle to help provide for his family, and his constant fear of the gangs in the area. On top of all of this, he still felt compelled to continue going to school. I don't know how much help I provided this boy, but after my conversation with him, it was clear to me the type of profession I needed to pursue: one of service to others…and honestly, I'm glad I did because all the money in the world would not make me happy if I lost sight of helping those around me."

Dillon smiled. "I don't know, Mr. Rice, all the money in the world would be pretty nice."

The counselor gave a small smirk. "Agreed."

Another small silence ensued as Dillon took a moment to let the lesson sink in. Dillon felt he had been of service to others in high school; he did volunteer work at the local hospital almost every weekend. The part of the phrase that was bothering him was "with a selfless heart."

How can I always think about others? Who will look out for me?

Dillon thought about asking Mr. Rice the questions he was thinking, but they sounded selfish.

Maybe that is the point. Maybe I shouldn't be thinking like that at all.

Mr. Rice broke the silence. "Dillon, have you ever heard of Mother Theresa?"

"Yes."

"How about Abraham Lincoln?"

Dillon laughed. "Of course."

"It's funny to me that Mother Theresa and Abraham Lincoln lived very different lives. Mother Theresa lived her entire life in poverty just like the boy in El Salvador, and Abraham Lincoln was the President of the United States. Why that is funny to me is that they both had the same goal in mind, to serve others to the best of their ability. You know as well as I do that they went about serving others in very different ways, but when service is the primary thought on one's mind, it is very difficult to go wrong."

Dillon nodded. "But what if other people ask me for more than I can give?"

Mr. Rice gave an understanding nod back. "It's equally as important to realize when others are thinking only of themselves. It's okay to say 'no' sometimes; most likely, you are not called to give everything you have like Mother Theresa did." He shot Dillon a quick smile as he had just compared Dillon to Mother Theresa, then continued seriously. "People may take advantage of you. People may try to use you. But at the end of the day, you cannot shut out everyone because of the misguided intentions of a few. Your life will be much more fulfilling if you consistently look to serve others with a selfless heart."

Dillon knew there were a million more ways he could have helped others when he was in high school, and he thought about some of the ways he could help others moving forward.

The counselor did not break eye contact. "That is my lesson, and this is the last thing I'll say. Sometimes, you try hard to serve others, but they do not accept your help."

Dillon's thoughts turned immediately to Will as his counselor spoke with a sympathetic look.

"Sometimes, Dillon, there is nothing more you can do."

For some reason, the comment did not move Dillon to tears or incite a lot of emotions. Dillon felt as though he finally understood how the lessons fit together.

I can't always keep others from doing stupid stuff, but I can make an effort to live as smart as possible. I can't force others to take action, but I can be decisive and move forward. I can't insist that others be persistent, but I can persevere. And I can't make others accept my service, but I can always offer.

Dillon also began to realize that he had only been thinking of his college decision when trying to understand his direction. He started to see that the lessons all spoke to a much deeper message about the direction he should go.

Forward.

Dillon felt much more comfortable. He took a deep breath, and looked at his counselor.

"Thanks, Mr. Rice."

"You're welcome. Here, I have this paper for you." Mr. Rice took a paper similar to all the others out of his pocket. "I decided not to write my lesson on it, but to leave it as a space for you. If you ever feel down and out, write what you are feeling on this paper. Sometimes you need to just write out your thoughts as a way to release some of the emotions you hold. I can't guarantee you'll feel better, but it is my final way to show you that this lesson is not about talking; it is about listening. It is not about my words; it is about your words. It is about serving with a selfless heart."

Dillon took the paper and shook Mr. Rice's hand. As Dillon turned to leave, Mr. Rice spoke one last time in his calm yet serious tone.

"One lesson left, Dillon. Enjoy."

Dillon nodded, turned the door handle, and walked out of the classroom. His phone rang in his pocket, but he ignored it.

Not wasting any time, Dillon unfolded the piece of paper from Mr. Rice as he walked toward the stairs.

Lesson Four
I Will Serve Others with a Selfless Heart

Feel free to use this space for anything you need.

Power of Will

Dillon pushed the piece of paper into his pocket. He felt the other papers taking up space, and he thought back to all the lessons. Initially, the entire day was troubling for him to accept, but he felt as though the lessons were finally coming together, and that he was much more in control of his circumstances.

Much more in control than the past few months at least.

Dillon walked out the doors of the business building just as he had a few hours earlier with Mayor Davis. The walkway toward the Joan of Arc chapel looked much more serene this time.

All of the lessons, Dillon knew, could make a real impact on his life. He reviewed them in his head as he walked.

I will not do stupid stuff.

I will always take action.

I will have unwavering persistence.

I will serve others with a selfless heart.

He added one more in his mind.

My direction is forward.

All of these lessons provided simple guidelines for how to live a successful and fulfilling life.

I wonder what the last lesson will be.

Dillon looked up and smiled as he spotted Martin looking down from a window in a building to Dillon's right. Martin gave Dillon a nod with a half-smile on his face. Despite the small smile, Dillon saw it was a serious nod as if there was some finality in it. Dillon shook off the thought and gave an appreciative nod back. Dillon glanced at the ground for a moment, and in looking back up, Martin was gone.

Dillon's feet moved him slowly toward his last lesson. He looked down at his schedule, and until this point, he hadn't realized that he would be receiving his last lesson inside the Joan of Arc chapel.

The garden in front of the chapel was bright and glowing just as it had been when he was walking with Martin earlier. Dillon took the time to take in the scenery as he slowly moved toward the chapel.

Marquette's campus was still empty. Dillon took a breath in realizing that the absence of people was actually a nice way for him to be alone for a while with his thoughts. The quiet really helped him internalize the information he had been given.

Maybe I should spend a little alone time outside of this experience just to think.

Dillon reached the front of the Joan of Arc chapel and looked up at the wooden doors that had been carefully carved so long ago and the tan brick that was covered in vines and ivy. He remembered hearing once that this chapel was the oldest building in the United States still used for its original purpose.

This is an interesting place.

Dillon didn't need to check his schedule again to know he was in the right place. As he put his hand on the metal handle, he had flashbacks from other moments in the day. Martin was right that he would never forget playing basketball with Dwyane Wade while learning from Coach Z, or seeing his grandmother with a large rifle; he'd never forget walking through a large crowd with Mayor Davis while the mayor's focus remained solely on him, and he would never forget Mr. Rice being there for him when he needed it.

What could the last lesson be?

Dillon's curiosity was getting the best of him, so he tightened his grip on the metal door handle and slowly pushed.

Dillon's jaw could have hit the ground as a stream of emotions flew through his mind. Confusion. Shock. Excitement. Surprise. Because standing at the front of the chapel, with a smug smile on his face, was Will.

"What's up, man? You're looking like you've seen a ghost!" Will laughed. He was wearing dark blue jeans and a white button-down shirt. His face, haircut, and general demeanor were exactly as Dillon remembered them.

Dillon frowned and his eyebrows furrowed; he wasn't sure how to respond.

This can't be real.

Dillon slowly moved around the chairs that made up the center of the chapel. There were only about twenty seats, as the chapel was not meant for large crowds. The chapel was dimly lit, and the original bricks making up the walls caused the area to be somewhat cooler than outside. Dillon didn't pay much attention to the faded stained glass windows or the chandelier holding candles because he was too stunned by the presence of Will. He cautiously stepped closer to the front with a look of bewilderment and disbelief.

Will didn't take offense to his friend's not-so-welcoming stare. "Come on up here. I only get so much time to see that crazy little hairdo of yours." Will laughed again as if there was nothing strange about the situation.

Dillon spoke slowly, still more confused than anything. "You're...dead."

"I knew you'd bring that up." Will pretended to be upset. "It's like we can't have one nice conversation without talking about it!" Will smiled, and after a short pause, continued in a somewhat more serious tone. "Martin told you that you would need to keep an open mind; that today would be a day you would never forget."

"But…how?"

Will straightened his posture, pretended to fix a bow tie, and did his best Martin impression. "Did I just hear you ask 'how'? Keep an open mind, Dillon."

The impression caused Dillon to smile a little bit, but he was still dumbfounded by the fact that Will was standing right in front of him.

"Alright, Dillon, its time for you to make a decision. Are you going to stay bewildered during this whole lesson and not appreciate this time we have together? Because I think you should suspend your disbelief, just for a while, put a smile on your face, and enjoy it, punk."

This drew a small smile from Dillon. It seemed like an easy decision, but it was hard for Dillon to suspend his disbelief. He did his best to push all of the questions he had to the back of his mind. "You have to admit, this is pretty strange."

Will laughed. "Life is always strange, this is just on the high end of the bell curve."

Now Dillon fully smiled. He had no idea what to think, but he had to admit, even if it was just to himself, that it was nice to see his best friend again. Questions were creeping back into his mind, but he didn't have time to ask as Will spoke first.

"Everyone's been telling me that you've been having a tough time lately, but I tell them that you'll be fine after a while." Will always seemed light-hearted when he talked; he always wore a smug smile as if the conversation was completely casual. "Do you know why I tell them that?"

Dillon didn't say anything. He was still pretty overwhelmed by the whole situation.

Will continued. "I tell them that you'll be fine because people are meant to be happy, and that you would eventually make the choice to be happy too."

Unsure of where this was going, Dillon interjected. "Is this part of my lesson?"

Will laughed. "So impatient! But yes, Dillon. Since you asked, it is your lesson. Choose to be happy. You can't always choose what situation you are placed in; in fact, you can rarely choose what happens to you, but you can always choose how you react. Most people get upset so easily; someone cuts them off while driving, and they are agitated for the rest of the day. It's so ridiculous that we let the smallest things define our happiness when we could simply let it go and choose to be happy."

Dillon looked at his friend. "It must be easy for you to say...being in heaven. Man, if heaven is different for everyone, I definitely didn't see yours being a chapel!"

Will laughed again. "Dillon's sense of humor is back!"

Dillon smiled, but thought for a moment and continued. "All I'm saying is, sometimes it isn't just little things that affect happiness. I lost my best friend."

"You can always choose to be happy. Grieving is one thing. I'm not saying you'll never feel down or sad, that's a natural part of life, but you can choose to say 'enough is enough' and move forward with a positive outlook."

My direction is forward.

Will then smiled wide, "I was thinking about the pranks we could have pulled on this campus..."

Dillon laughed, "Like what?"

"Think about the possibilities! You're surrounded by eight thousand people your age; you could sneak hot sauce into cafeteria food or use zip ties to lock people in dorm rooms!"

Dillon had to admit, it would be pretty funny, but he knew he could get in some serious trouble for doing those things.

Will put a serious look on his face again; he always had a feel for the perfect balance of serious and fun. Thinking back, this was one of the things that Dillon liked most about

Will. "Honest question. Do you think I would have wanted you to mope around after I died?"

He's dead.

The thought came back to Dillon, and it was very difficult for him to answer the question, but Will interjected anyway.

"I think you know as well as I do that I would have wanted you to move forward and be happy. I know how difficult it can be, but I thought it was important that I told you. I want you to be happy."

Dillon nodded. "Thanks, Will."

Will smiled. "Because it *kills* me to see you like this!"

Even though it was probably the worst joke Dillon had ever heard, he couldn't help but smile.

"So that's the lesson. Keep smiling. Move forward. Be happy." He took a folded piece of paper out of his front pocket. "I'll give you this, but I'm sure this is a lesson you can remember."

Dillon took the piece of paper and smiled. He thought for a moment about Martin.

I definitely will never forget this.

Dillon looked up at Will. "Hey Will, is there a heaven?"

Will smiled. "You bet there is."

There was a small silence before Will spoke, "I wish we had more time…but I have to go. It was great to see you; I know that you will be happy."

Now tears started to well in Dillon's eyes, but he did his best to hold them in. The last time he lost Will he didn't know it was coming. Thinking about losing him again was hurting Dillon, but in the back of his mind, he knew that he was going to be all right. He knew that all of the lessons he had learned today could dramatically change his life if he chose to make all five simple decisions every day.

I will not do stupid stuff.

I will take action.

I will have unwavering persistence.

I will serve others with a selfless heart.
I will choose to be happy.

Dillon didn't know what to say as Will walked toward the back of the church. Before exiting, he turned around. "Hey Dillon…" Will took his lucky coin out of his pocket and flipped it across the chapel. "I'm not going to be needing this anymore. Maybe it will bring you some luck in college."

Dillon smiled, catching the coin with both hands. "Thanks, Will."

They exchanged a nod, and with that, Will turned and walked out of the chapel.

Dillon sat down in the front row of the small chapel with so many questions left in his head. He rubbed his thumb over the smooth piece of paper that Will had given him. After seeing Will, the events of the day seemed much more strange.

Why has no one else been on campus all day?
How did Will come talk to me face-to-face?
Is any of this real?

Scanning the chapel, Dillon did something he hadn't done since Will's death; he bowed his head, folded his hands, and said a short prayer.

I don't know where my life is headed, but please guide me. I know I can follow these lessons much easier with your help.

Dillon unfolded his hands and slowly peeled open the piece of paper Will had given him.

Lesson Five
I Will Choose to be Happy

Today, I will choose to be happy. I will take the high road and not let negative thoughts and feelings control my life. While I realize grief and sadness are normal emotions, I will look to move forward as time progresses and not dwell on the negative aspects of my past.

I will work to instill happiness in the people around me. I will stay positive especially when dealing with challenging situations. Although I am aware that the people around me may often complain or focus on only the negatives, I will make the choice to put a positive spin on any situation.

I will never allow the trying moments in my life to define who I am; only I can define who I am. The difficult times in my life will help shape my perspective and mold my character.

There is no substitute for a positive attitude. I see and understand the enormous impact it can have on an everyday basis. So, today I will not dwell on the negatives; I will consciously stay positive, I will work to move forward, and I will choose to be happy.

Homework:

Choose to be happy every day.

Moving Forward

Dillon took a deep breath and stood up. He walked toward the back of the chapel, where Will had left just minutes ago and stood by the door. He gave a reminiscent look back to the front of the chapel where he had just had a reunion with his best friend. While it was good to see Will, there were a million more questions in Dillon's mind.

Opening the door of the chapel, the sun made Dillon squint, and the radiance of the flowers was close-to overwhelming. Dillon took a glance around and, remembering Will's lesson, put a small smile on his face.

As he stood, Dillon's pocket started to vibrate, and his phone began to ring. He reached into his pocket, feeling like he had ignored his phone for long enough. He didn't recognize the number of whoever it was that had been calling him all day, but he decided to answer this time.

Dillon pulled the phone up to his ear. "Hello?"

Then the world went black.

A beeping sound stayed constant and didn't help the pounding in Dillon's head. His eyes were shut, and he felt himself lying down on a bed that was not exactly soft. He slowly pried his eyes open and scanned the dimly lit hospital room. He was alone in the room with a heart monitor consistently beeping next to him.

What is going on? Was this all a dream?

Dillon's mother walked into the room. She looked tired and her eyes were red as if she'd been crying. She seemed surprised to see her son awake. "Hey…" she said with a sympathetic smile.

"What's going on?"

"How are you feeling? Are you okay?"

Dillon was more confused than ever.

Where am I? How did I get here?

Dillon couldn't remember. He asked his mother again. "What's going on?"

"You went to pick up Will, and the two of you were hit by a drunk driver."

What? How long have I been in this hospital bed?

His mother had a look of concern, "Are you feeling okay?"

Dillon looked toward the wall too disoriented to respond.

His mother grabbed his hand. "Dillon, it's about Will." She looked down at the ground. "He passed away in the accident."

Dillon couldn't understand what was happening. He scrunched his eyebrows in confusion. "I know."

The comment seemed to confuse Dillon's mother as well. "What?"

"I know he did. Why are you telling me this now?"

His mother had a troubled look. Dillon couldn't understand. Everything had been far too real for him to accept that it was all a dream.

The people. The lessons. The emotions.

Seeing that he needed a second to process everything, his mother spoke. "I'm going to go get the nurse, okay? Do you need anything?"

Dillon shook his head, and his mom turned toward the door. Before exiting, she turned around, "If you're feeling up to it, you had some visitors while you were...out." She gestured to a small stack of "Get Well Soon" cards on the table near the bed. "The doctor told them that talking to you might be beneficial. They all left really nice notes." She nodded her head, then smiled and moved into the hallway.

Not sure what to think, Dillon sat up in the bed and reached for the small stack of cards on the table.

Could they really all have come and talked to me? What did they say?

Glancing at each card, he smiled as he found one from Coach Z, one from Mayor Davis, one from his grandmother, and one from Mr. Rice. He thought back to the lessons he had learned from them, and he knew they were lessons he would keep at the center of his life.

But one lesson is missing.

As he slowly moved to place the stack of cards back on the table, something dropped from the pile onto his lap. Looking down, Dillon saw the object that had fallen from within the cards; it was Will's lucky coin.

He couldn't help but smile.

There it is.

At that moment, his mom walked back into the room with a man in a white doctor's coat. The man had a clipboard in one hand and a pen in the other. He scribbled something onto the clipboard, checked his watch, then looked up, "How are you feeling, Dillon?"

"I'm feeling alright, Martin, how are you?"

Everything is going to be all right.

ABOUT THE AUTHOR
KYLE WILLKOM
@KyleWillkom, @FOCUS_Kyle

Kyle Willkom is a Brand Manager, Keynote Speaker, and Leadership Trainer for a leadership development company called FOCUS Training. He works to spread brand awareness through online channels and travels throughout North America delivering keynote speeches and running interactive workshops.

Kyle Willkom grew up in the small town of Marshfield, Wisconsin, home of the World's Largest Round Barn and the World's Largest Urinal.

He is a graduate of Marquette University with degrees in Marketing and Entrepreneurship. While at Marquette, Kyle had a wide range of experiences: he spent a year training with the Army ROTC and two semesters as a manager of Marquette Men's Basketball; he was elected vice president of his dorm and the president of a student business organization called the Go-Getters; he even started a musical comedy rap group called the Spanish Odonnells!

Kyle loves interacting with new people. He'd be excited to hear from you on Twitter and on his Facebook page!

Contact Information:

Kyle Willkom
www.KyleWillkom.com
Kyle.Willkom@gmail.com

Kyle Willkom's speaking inspires groups to take action, lead by example, and embrace the five lessons within this book. His energy and insight keep audiences laughing while they learn.

Contact FOCUS Training to book Kyle Willkom to speak at your next event!

FOCUS Training, Inc.
(877) 273-4670
Info@focustraining.com
531 S. Water St.
Milwaukee, WI 53204

Be sure to:

* Follow @FOCUS_Kyle and @KyleWillkom on Twitter

* Like the Kyle Willkom Facebook Page

* Visit www.KyleWillkom.com

Made in the USA
Lexington, KY
17 December 2013